CW00545204

TABLE OF CONT

WELCOME TO ECUADOR

As I stepped off the plane, I could already feel the vibrant energy of Ecuador enveloping me. The air was thick with the scent of tropical flora, and the distant sound of lively music filled my ears. I had heard tales of this enchanting country, and now it was time for me to embark on my own adventure.

My journey began in Quito, the capital city nestled high in the Andes Mountains. The narrow, cobblestone streets led me through a maze of colonial architecture, each building exuding a sense of history and charm. I couldn't help but be captivated by the intricate details of the ornate churches that lined the city, their spires reaching towards the heavens.

One particular morning, I found myself standing in awe at the base of the towering statue of the Virgin of El Panecillo, which overlooked the city. The panoramic view of Quito's sprawling landscape took my breath away. The vibrant colors of the buildings, the bustling market squares, and the emerald-green hills in the distance were all a testament to the beauty of Ecuador.

The adventure continued as I ventured into the Amazon Rainforest. With a knowledgeable guide by my side, I trekked through dense foliage, my senses heightened by the symphony of chirping birds and the rustle of unseen creatures. I marveled at the sheer diversity of life around me, from the vividly colored butterflies to the elusive monkeys swinging through the treetops.

One evening, as the sun began to set, I found myself in the Galapagos Islands, a place teeming with unique wildlife found nowhere else on Earth. I embarked on a snorkeling adventure, diving into the crystal-clear waters to swim alongside playful sea lions and graceful sea turtles. The underwater world was a kaleidoscope of vibrant corals and mesmerizing fish, an experience that left me in awe of the incredible biodiversity that Ecuador has to offer.

But it wasn't just the natural wonders that captured my heart. It was the warmth and hospitality of the

Ecuadorian people that truly made my experience unforgettable. Everywhere I went, I was greeted with smiles and open arms, their pride in their country evident in their conversations and laughter. Whether it was sharing a meal with a local family, dancing to traditional music at a lively fiesta, or simply engaging in friendly banter with market vendors, I felt a genuine connection to the people and their culture.

As my time in Ecuador drew to a close, I reflected on the myriad of experiences I had been fortunate enough to encounter. From the towering mountains to the pristine beaches, from the bustling cities to the serene countryside, this country had taken me on a journey that awakened my senses and nourished my soul.

Ecuador, with its rich biodiversity, captivating landscapes, and vibrant culture, had left an indelible mark on my heart. It was a place where adventure met tranquility, where the beauty of nature intertwined with the warmth of its people.

So, if you ever find yourself in Ecuador, be prepared to have your senses awakened, your spirit rejuvenated, and your heart forever touched. Welcome to Ecuador, where every step you take is a step towards an unforgettable experience.

Discovering Ecuador: A Land of Magic and Wonder

Ecuador, a country nestled in the heart of South America, is a land of magic and wonder that never fails to captivate the adventurous soul. From its diverse landscapes to its rich cultural heritage, this enchanting country offers a plethora of experiences that leave visitors in awe.

As I embarked on my journey through Ecuador, I was greeted by the breathtaking beauty of its natural wonders. The majestic peaks of the Andes Mountains stood tall, their snow-capped summits reaching for the heavens. I found myself trekking through lush valleys, surrounded by cascading waterfalls and vibrant wildflowers that painted the landscape in a kaleidoscope of colors.

My exploration led me to the renowned Galapagos Islands, a haven of unique wildlife and pristine beaches. As I embarked on a boat tour, I encountered playful sea lions lounging on volcanic rocks, graceful sea turtles gliding through the turquoise waters, and exotic birds soaring through the clear blue skies. The Galapagos Islands were a living laboratory of evolution, where nature's wonders unfolded before my eyes.

Venturing into the Amazon Rainforest was like stepping into a mythical realm. The dense foliage whispered secrets of ancient civilizations, while the symphony of exotic birds and primates echoed through the trees. My senses were heightened as I embarked on a canoe ride along the winding rivers, observing elusive creatures hidden in the depths of the jungle. The Amazon was a sanctuary of biodiversity, where every step revealed a new marvel of nature.

But Ecuador's magic extended beyond its natural wonders. Its rich cultural heritage added another layer of fascination to my journey. In the charming colonial cities, such as Quito and Cuenca, I walked through cobblestone streets lined with colorful buildings, each one telling a story of a bygone era. I immersed myself in the vibrant traditions of indigenous communities, witnessing their vibrant festivals and intricate craftsmanship.

Ecuador was a land where ancient traditions and modern influences harmoniously coexisted. From the lively markets filled with handicrafts and fresh produce to the mouthwatering flavors of traditional cuisine, every encounter was a celebration of the country's diverse heritage.

As my time in Ecuador came to an end, I realized that this land of magic and wonder had not only left an indelible mark on my soul but had also awakened a newfound appreciation for the beauty and diversity of our planet. Ecuador had invited me to explore, to marvel, and to embrace the unknown. It has taught me that there is enchantment in every corner of the world, waiting to be discovered by those willing to embark on the journey.

Ecuador's History and Culture

Ecuador's history is a tapestry woven with the threads of ancient civilizations, colonial influences, and a rich indigenous heritage. The country's cultural diversity is a testament to its fascinating past.

The land that is now Ecuador was once home to the indigenous civilizations of the Inca, the Cañari, and the Quitu. These advanced societies left behind impressive architectural marvels, such as the Incan ruins of Ingapirca, and a legacy of art and craftsmanship that can still be seen in the traditional designs and textiles of modern-day Ecuador.

The arrival of the Spanish in the 16th century brought about a significant transformation in Ecuador's cultural landscape. The colonial period left an indelible mark on the country, as Spanish influences merged with indigenous traditions. Colonial cities like Quito and Cuenca became centers of architectural grandeur, with their well-preserved colonial buildings and churches showcasing a unique blend of European and indigenous architectural styles.

Today, Ecuador celebrates its cultural heritage through vibrant festivals, music, and art. The Inti Raymi, or Festival of the Sun, is a colorful celebration of indigenous traditions that takes place in various regions of the country. Traditional music, such as the lively rhythms of the marimba and the soul-stirring melodies of the Andean flute, can be heard during these festivities and in everyday life.

Ecuador's cuisine is also a reflection of its diverse cultural heritage. From the hearty dishes of the highlands, such as llapingachos (potato pancakes) and hornado (roast pork), to the seafood delights of the coastal regions, including ceviche and encocado (coconut-based seafood stew), Ecuadorian cuisine tantalizes the taste buds with a fusion of flavors.

Overview of Ecuador

The country is divided into four distinct regions: the Sierra (highlands), the Costa (coastal region), the Oriente (Amazon Rainforest), and the Galapagos Islands. Each region offers unique experiences and attractions.

In the Sierra, visitors can explore the colonial cities of Quito and Cuenca, with their well-preserved architecture and rich history. They can also embark on thrilling adventures in the Andes Mountains, hiking through picturesque valleys and encountering indigenous communities along the way.

The coastal region, known as the Costa, boasts stunning beaches and vibrant beach towns like Montañita and

Salinas. Here, visitors can indulge in water sports, relax on sun-kissed shores, and savor delicious seafood delicacies.

The Oriente, Ecuador's slice of the Amazon Rainforest, is a paradise for nature enthusiasts. Exploring the dense jungle, visitors can encounter unique wildlife, interact with indigenous communities, and navigate the winding rivers that crisscross the region.

And then there are the Galapagos Islands, a UNESCO World Heritage site and a living laboratory of evolution. These remote islands offer unrivaled opportunities for wildlife encounters, where visitors can observe species found nowhere else on the planet.

Ecuador's cultural heritage is just as captivating as its natural beauty. The country is a melting pot of indigenous traditions and colonial influences, reflected in its vibrant festivals, art, and cuisine.

CHAPTER 1: INTRODUCTION TO ECUADOR

Ecuador is a country that beckons with its incredible biodiversity, stunning landscapes, and vibrant culture. With a rich history and a diverse population, Ecuador offers a captivating introduction to the wonders of this extraordinary region.

Ecuador is known for its diverse geography, from the soaring peaks of the Andes Mountains to the lush Amazon Rainforest and the pristine beaches along its Pacific coastline. This variety of landscapes allows visitors to embark on thrilling adventures, whether it's trekking through high-altitude trails, exploring the dense jungle, or relaxing on sun-drenched shores.

The country's cultural heritage is equally captivating. Indigenous traditions are deeply ingrained in Ecuadorian society, with vibrant festivals, colorful markets, and traditional crafts showcasing the customs and craftsmanship of its people. The colonial influence can be seen in the well-preserved architecture of cities like Quito and Cuenca, where cobblestone streets and ornate churches transport visitors back in time.

Ecuador is also home to the awe-inspiring Galapagos Islands, a haven of unique wildlife and pristine natural beauty. This archipelago, made famous by Charles Darwin's studies, offers unparalleled opportunities for close encounters with remarkable species found nowhere else on Earth.

Brief History of Ecuador

Ecuador's history is a fascinating tapestry that weaves together ancient civilizations, colonial influences, and struggles for independence. The land that is now Ecuador has been inhabited for thousands of years, with indigenous cultures such as the Inca, Cañari, and Quitu leaving their mark on the region.

The arrival of the Spanish in the 16th century marked a pivotal turning point in Ecuador's history. The area became part of the Viceroyalty of Peru, and Spanish colonizers established cities and encomiendas, exploiting the native population and extracting valuable resources.

In the early 19th century, Ecuador, along with other South American colonies, fought for independence from Spain. The liberation movement was led by notable figures such as Simón Bolívar and Antonio José de Sucre. Ecuador gained its independence in 1822 and briefly became part of Gran Colombia, a federation that included present-day Colombia, Venezuela, and Panama.

In 1830, Ecuador became a separate nation, and throughout the following centuries, the country experienced political instability and territorial disputes. It faced border conflicts with neighboring countries, including Peru and Colombia. Additionally, Ecuador saw a series of military coups and political upheavals.

In recent years, Ecuador has made strides towards stability and democratic governance. The country has embraced its rich cultural heritage, celebrating indigenous traditions and promoting cultural diversity.

Weather in Ecuador

Ecuador's unique location near the equator gives it a varied climate that is influenced by its diverse geography. Despite its small size, the country boasts a wide range of microclimates, offering something for every type of weather enthusiast.

Ecuador can be broadly divided into three regions: the Sierra (highlands), the Costa (coastal region), and the Oriente (Amazon Rainforest). Each region experiences distinct weather patterns.

In the Sierra, the weather is characterized by mild temperatures year-round, with cooler temperatures in the higher elevations. Quito, the capital city located in the Sierra, enjoys spring-like weather throughout the year, with average temperatures ranging from 50 to 70 degrees Fahrenheit (10 to 21 degrees Celsius). However, weather can vary greatly within a short distance due to the varied topography.

On the coastal region, the Costa, the weather is influenced by ocean currents and prevailing winds. It experiences a tropical climate with higher temperatures and humidity compared to the Sierra. The coastal cities of Guayaquil and Manta have average temperatures ranging from 75 to 90 degrees Fahrenheit (24 to 32 degrees Celsius) with high levels of humidity.

In the Oriente, the Amazon Rainforest region, the weather is hot and humid throughout the year, with frequent rainfall. The temperatures can reach 90 degrees Fahrenheit (32 degrees Celsius) or higher, and rainfall is common due to the region's tropical rainforest climate.

It's important to note that Ecuador's weather can vary significantly depending on the elevation and proximity to the coast or rainforest. Travelers are advised to check the specific weather conditions for their desired destinations and pack accordingly.

Best Time to Visit Ecuador

Choosing the best time to visit Ecuador depends on your preferences and the specific regions you plan to explore. Due to its varied geography and microclimates, Ecuador offers favorable conditions throughout the year for different activities and destinations.

The dry season, which generally runs from June to September, is considered the best time to visit the Galapagos Islands. During this period, the weather is pleasant, with cooler temperatures and clear skies. It's an ideal time for wildlife observation, snorkeling, and diving, as the waters are calmer and visibility is excellent.

If you plan to explore the Andean highlands, including cities like Quito and Cuenca, the dry season from June to September is also recommended. This period offers mild temperatures, less rainfall, and clearer skies, making it ideal for hiking, sightseeing, and cultural experiences.

For those interested in visiting the Amazon Rainforest, the dry season from December to March is a good time. Although rain is still common, the water levels are lower, making it easier to navigate the rivers and explore the dense jungle.

The coastal region, including cities like Guayaquil and Manta, has a tropical climate and is generally hot and humid throughout the year. However, the dry season from December to April offers more stable weather, with less rainfall and sunny days, making it ideal for beach activities and water sports.

Transportation in Ecuador and Airport Information

When it comes to transportation in Ecuador, travelers have various options to navigate the country and explore its diverse regions. From domestic flights to buses and taxis, there are reliable means of transportation available to suit different preferences and budgets.

For those arriving by air, Ecuador has several international airports. The busiest airport is Mariscal Sucre International Airport (UIO) located near Quito, the capital city. It serves as a major gateway for international flights and offers connections to various destinations within Ecuador. Another significant airport is José Joaquín de Olmedo International Airport (GYE) in Guayaquil, the largest city in Ecuador. It provides convenient access to the southern coastal region.

Within Ecuador, domestic flights are a popular choice for traveling long distances quickly. TAME and LATAM are two of the main airlines that operate domestic flights, connecting major cities such as Quito, Guayaquil, Cuenca, and the Galapagos Islands. Domestic flights offer a time-efficient way to explore the country, especially for travelers with limited time.

Buses are a common mode of transportation in Ecuador and are widely used for both short and long-distance travel. The country has an extensive bus network that connects cities, towns, and rural areas. Buses range from basic to luxury coaches, with various comfort levels and amenities available. This option allows travelers to experience the scenic beauty of Ecuador's landscapes while connecting with local communities.

Taxis are readily available in most cities and towns, providing a convenient way to get around. In larger cities like Quito and Guayaquil, taxis are metered, while in smaller towns, negotiated fares are common. It's advisable to ensure that the taxi has a working meter or agree on a price before starting the journey.

For inter-island travel to the Galapagos Islands, flights are the primary mode of transportation. Flights depart from Quito or Guayaquil to either Baltra Island or San Cristobal Island. Local transportation on the islands mainly consists of taxis, buses, and boats for exploring different sites.

7 Reasons to Plan your Trip to Ecuador as your next Vacation Destination

With its natural wonders, cultural treasures, adventure opportunities, and warm hospitality, Ecuador is an ideal vacation destination that offers something for everyone. Whether you seek adventure, relaxation, or a cultural immersion, Ecuador promises an unforgettable journey that will leave you with cherished memories for years to come. Here are 7 reasons to plan your visit to Ecuador:

1. Breathtaking Natural Beauty: Ecuador is a paradise for nature lovers, boasting diverse

landscapes that include the towering Andes Mountains, lush Amazon Rainforest, pristine beaches, and the iconic Galapagos Islands. From hiking through stunning national parks to snorkeling with exotic marine life, Ecuador offers an array of natural wonders that will leave you awe-struck.

2. Cultural Richness: Immerse yourself in Ecuador's vibrant culture and heritage. Explore the charming colonial cities of Quito and Cuenca, where cobblestone streets, colorful markets, and historic buildings reflect the country's fascinating history. Engage with indigenous communities and witness their traditional rituals, crafts, and festivals, gaining a deeper appreciation for Ecuador's diverse cultural tapestry.

3. Galapagos Islands: A trip to Ecuador is incomplete without visiting the world-renowned Galapagos Islands. These isolated islands are home to unique wildlife found nowhere else on the planet. Witness giant tortoises, marine iguanas, playful sea lions, and an incredible array of bird species up close, as you explore this living laboratory of evolution.

4. Adventure and Outdoor Activities: Ecuador is a playground for adventure seekers. Embark on thrilling activities like hiking the Quilotoa Loop, rafting down the rivers of the Amazon Rainforest, zip-lining through cloud forests, or surfing the Pacific waves. With its diverse landscapes, Ecuador offers endless opportunities for adrenaline-pumping adventures.

5. Culinary Delights: Indulge in Ecuador's flavorful cuisine, which showcases a fusion of indigenous, Spanish, and African influences. Sample delicious dishes such as ceviche (marinated seafood), llapingachos (potato pancakes), and locro de papas (potato soup), while savoring the rich flavors and fresh ingredients that make Ecuadorian cuisine so enticing.

6. Wildlife and Birdwatching: Ecuador is a paradise for wildlife enthusiasts and birdwatchers. Beyond the Galapagos, the mainland offers ample opportunities to spot a wide variety of species. Explore the cloud forests of Mindo, where hummingbirds and colorful toucans abound, or venture into the Amazon Rainforest to encounter monkeys, sloths, and an array of exotic birds.

7. Warm Hospitality: Experience the warmth and friendliness of the Ecuadorian people. From the bustling markets to remote communities, locals are known for their welcoming nature, making you feel right at home during your visit. Interact with locals, share stories, and embrace the hospitality that will leave a lasting impression.

CHAPTER 2: EXPLORING ECUADOR'S NATURAL WONDERS

Ecuador is a country of astonishing natural beauty, where diverse landscapes and ecosystems converge to create a haven for outdoor enthusiasts and nature lovers. From the towering peaks of the Andes Mountains to the lush rainforests of the Amazon, and the enchanting Galapagos Islands, Ecuador is a treasure trove of natural wonders waiting to be explored.

The Andes Mountains dominate the country's landscape, offering breathtaking vistas and thrilling adventures. Hike through the misty cloud forests, encounter snow-capped volcanoes, and traverse picturesque valleys dotted with indigenous communities. The Avenue of the Volcanoes, a stretch of the Andean highlands, showcases Ecuador's volcanic beauty, where mountains like Cotopaxi and Chimborazo rise majestically.

Venturing into the Amazon Rainforest, visitors are immersed in a world of unparalleled biodiversity. Explore the dense jungles teeming with exotic wildlife, listen to the symphony of birdcalls, and navigate the winding rivers that meander through this verdant paradise. Encounter playful monkeys, vibrant macaws, and elusive jaguars as you delve into the heart of the Amazon.

No visit to Ecuador would be complete without experiencing the Galapagos Islands, a UNESCO World Heritage site and a living laboratory of evolution. These remote islands offer a unique opportunity to witness wildlife found nowhere else on Earth. Observe the iconic Galapagos tortoises, marvel at the colorful marine life while snorkeling, and witness the courtship dances of the famous blue-footed boobies.

Andean Highlands: Volcanoes and Scenic Landscapes

The Andean Highlands of Ecuador offer a captivating blend of dramatic volcanic peaks, pristine lakes, and picturesque valleys. This awe-inspiring region is a paradise for outdoor enthusiasts and nature lovers, promising unforgettable adventures and breathtaking vistas.

The Avenue of the Volcanoes, located in the central Andean region, is a prominent highlight of the Andean Highlands. This scenic stretch is home to a chain of majestic volcanoes, including the iconic Cotopaxi, Chimborazo, and Tungurahua. These towering peaks, often adorned with snow-capped summits, create a stunning backdrop that enthralls visitors.

Hiking and climbing opportunities abound in the Andean Highlands, attracting adventure seekers from around the world. Trek through the enchanting cloud forests, witness the vibrant biodiversity, and ascend to the heights of these volcanic giants for panoramic views that will leave you in awe.

In addition to the volcanoes, the Andean Highlands boast breathtaking landscapes that vary from turquoise crater lakes to verdant valleys. Explore the Quilotoa Crater Lake, a stunning natural wonder with its vibrant hues and picturesque surroundings. Journey through the fertile valleys of the Mindo Cloud Forest, where cascading waterfalls, hummingbirds, and diverse flora and fauna await.

Indigenous communities dot the Andean Highlands, offering a chance to immerse in local culture and traditions. Discover their way of life, witness traditional festivals, and explore colorful markets where handcrafted textiles and unique artisanal products are on display.

Cloud Forests: Mystical Beauty and Wildlife

Ecuador's cloud forests are enchanting and mystical realms that beckon travelers with their ethereal beauty and abundant biodiversity. Nestled in the misty mountains, these unique ecosystems are characterized by their lush vegetation, cool temperatures, and a shroud of mist that adds an air of mystery.

These forests are found in the higher elevations of the Andean region, where the moist air from the Amazon Rainforest collides with the cool air from the mountains. This collision creates a perfect environment for a rich diversity of plant and animal life to thrive.

Exploring Ecuador's cloud forests is like stepping into a fairy tale. Dense canopies of moss-covered trees, hanging orchids, and epiphytes create a magical atmosphere. Sunlight filters through the mist, creating an otherworldly ambiance that transports you into a realm of serenity and natural wonder.

The cloud forests are also home to an incredible array of wildlife. Colorful hummingbirds flit from flower to flower, while elusive creatures like the spectacled bear and the Andean cock-of-the-rock find refuge in the dense foliage. Birdwatchers will delight in the opportunity to spot rare species like the elusive Andean condor and the resplendent quetzal.

Hiking and trekking trails wind through the cloud forests, offering opportunities to explore this pristine ecosystem up close. Discover hidden waterfalls, encounter exotic bird species, and witness the captivating beauty of these mystical forests.

To fully immerse in the cloud forest experience, consider staying at eco-lodges that are committed to conservation and sustainable tourism. These lodges provide a unique opportunity to connect with nature and support local communities.

Coastal Regions: Beaches and Marine Life

Ecuador's coastal regions offer a stunning contrast to its highlands and rainforests, boasting a stretch of beautiful beaches and a rich marine ecosystem. With its Pacific coastline, this region entices visitors with its sun-soaked shores, vibrant coastal towns, and abundant marine life.

The coastal area is blessed with an array of beaches, catering to different preferences. From bustling resort towns like Salinas and Manta to secluded and pristine stretches of sand like Ayampe and Los Frailes, there's a beach for every taste. Whether you're seeking relaxation, water sports, or simply the joy of basking in the sun, Ecuador's coastal regions have it all.

But it's not just about the beaches. The Pacific waters along Ecuador's coast are teeming with marine life, making it a haven for snorkeling, diving, and whale-watching. The underwater world here is a kaleidoscope of colors, with vibrant coral reefs and a variety of fish species. Encounter playful sea lions, sea turtles, and rays as you explore the underwater realm.

The coastal region is also known for its delicious seafood. Sample mouthwatering ceviche, a popular local dish made from marinated seafood, and savor fresh shrimp, lobster, and fish delicacies that are a hallmark of Ecuadorian coastal cuisine.

Beyond the beaches, the coastal towns and cities have their own charm. Guayaquil, the largest city in Ecuador, offers a bustling atmosphere with its lively Malecon waterfront, modern architecture, and vibrant cultural scene. Explore the charming fishing villages along the coast, where you can witness the daily lives of fishermen and enjoy the tranquility of their surroundings.

Sierra Negra Volcano: Hiking and Volcanic Exploration

Sierra Negra Volcano, located in the Galapagos Islands of Ecuador, is a captivating destination for adventurers and nature enthusiasts. With its dramatic landscapes and unique geological features, this volcano offers a thrilling hiking experience and a glimpse into the fascinating world of volcanic activity.

Sierra Negra is one of the most active volcanoes in the Galapagos archipelago and is known for having one of the largest volcanic calderas in the world. The caldera measures about 10 kilometers in diameter, creating a vast and awe-inspiring expanse to explore.

Hiking to the summit of Sierra Negra provides breathtaking views of the volcanic landscape, with vistas that stretch as far as the eye can see. As you ascend, you'll witness the power and beauty of the volcanic formations, including lava fields, sulfur vents, and volcanic cones.

The highlight of the hike is reaching the rim of the caldera, where you can peer into the massive volcanic crater. The scale of the caldera is truly remarkable, and the sight of the barren landscape and volcanic formations is both humbling and mesmerizing.

The hike also offers opportunities to observe the unique flora and fauna of the Galapagos Islands. Keep an eye out for Galapagos giant tortoises, finches, and other endemic species that call this volcanic terrain home.

While the hike can be challenging, the rewards are well worth the effort. It's an opportunity to connect with nature in a raw and powerful way, to witness the forces that shape our planet, and to experience the volcanic heritage of the Galapagos Islands.

Yasuni National Park: Amazon Rainforest Conservation

Yasuni National Park, located in the heart of the Ecuadorian Amazon Rainforest, is a pristine and biodiverse haven that showcases the importance of conservation and sustainable practices. This protected area is a testament to Ecuador's commitment to preserving its natural treasures and promoting the ecological balance of the Amazon.

Yasuni is recognized as one of the most biodiverse places on Earth, boasting an extraordinary variety of plant and animal species. The park is home to numerous indigenous communities that have coexisted with the rainforest for centuries, preserving their traditional knowledge and harmonious relationship with nature.

Exploring Yasuni National Park is a mesmerizing journey into the heart of the Amazon. Hike through dense jungles, cruise along winding rivers, and navigate through flooded forests, all while being immersed in the sights and sounds of this lush ecosystem. Encounter towering trees, vibrant orchids, and exotic wildlife such as monkeys, sloths, and colorful bird species.

One of the park's unique features is the Yasuni ITT Initiative, which aims to protect the park's oil-rich underground reserves by promoting international cooperation and funding. This initiative prioritizes the preservation of the park's rich biodiversity, the rights of indigenous communities, and the mitigation of climate change.

Visitors to Yasuni have the opportunity to engage with local communities, learning about their sustainable practices, traditional medicine, and cultural heritage. Community-based ecotourism initiatives provide a chance to witness firsthand the importance of protecting and preserving the rainforest while supporting the livelihoods of local residents.

Yasuni National Park stands as a symbol of Ecuador's dedication to environmental conservation and sustainable development. It serves as a reminder of the immense value of the Amazon Rainforest and the urgent need to protect these precious ecosystems for future generations.

CHAPTER 3: EVENTS, ATTRACTION AND ITINERARY

Ecuador is a country that offers a diverse range of events, attractions, and experiences for travelers to enjoy. From vibrant cultural festivals to breathtaking natural wonders, there's something for everyone in this captivating South American nation.

Ecuador's calendar is filled with colorful and lively events that showcase the country's rich heritage and traditions. The Inti Raymi, or the Festival of the Sun, celebrated in June, is a mesmerizing display of indigenous rituals and dances that pay homage to the Inca sun god. Another must-see event is the Fiesta de la Mama Negra in Latacunga, a vibrant celebration blending Catholic and indigenous traditions, complete with parades, music, and costumes.

The country's attractions are equally captivating. Explore the historical center of Quito, a UNESCO World Heritage site, with its well-preserved colonial architecture and stunning churches. Discover the enchanting Galapagos Islands, where you can witness unique wildlife and the wonders of evolution. Visit the Mindo Cloud Forest, home to diverse bird species and thrilling zip-line adventures. And of course, no visit to

Ecuador is complete without exploring the majestic Andean peaks and the Amazon Rainforest.

Planning an itinerary in Ecuador allows you to experience the country's highlights and hidden gems. From the bustling markets of Otavalo to the picturesque colonial town of Cuenca, there's a wealth of destinations to explore. Whether you're seeking adventure, cultural immersion, or natural beauty, Ecuador offers a plethora of options to create an unforgettable travel experience.

Top 5 Events to Attend

Ecuador is a vibrant country that celebrates its rich cultural heritage through a variety of festivals and events. Attending these festivities offers a unique opportunity to immerse oneself in the local culture, witness traditional customs, and create lasting memories. Here are the top five events to experience in Ecuador:

1. Inti Raymi: Held in June, Inti Raymi is an ancient Inca festival that celebrates the sun god. It features colorful processions, traditional dances, and music in the historic city of Cuenca.

2. Fiesta de la Mama Negra: Taking place in Latacunga in November, this festival combines

Catholic and indigenous traditions. It showcases lively parades, vibrant costumes, and traditional rituals honoring the Virgen de la Merced.

3. Carnival: Celebrated across Ecuador in February or March, Carnival is a joyous and exuberant event. It includes water fights, parades, live music, and the crowning of a carnival queen.

4. Independence Day: On August 10th, Ecuador commemorates its independence from Spanish rule with patriotic parades, fireworks, concerts, and cultural performances throughout the country.

5. La Diablada de Píllaro: Taking place in the town of Pillaro in December, La Diablada is a unique event blending Catholic and indigenous traditions. Participants don elaborate devil costumes and masks, dancing through the streets to ward off evil spirits.

Attending these top five events in Ecuador allows visitors to witness the country's cultural diversity, connect with local traditions, and join in the festive spirit that permeates the nation.

Top 5 Attractions in Ecuador

Ecuador is a country blessed with stunning natural landscapes, rich cultural heritage, and unique biodiversity. From the enchanting Galapagos Islands to the awe-inspiring Andean highlands, there are countless attractions to explore. Here are the top five must-visit attractions in Ecuador:

1. Galapagos Islands: Known for their unrivaled biodiversity and the inspiration for Charles Darwin's theory of evolution, the Galapagos Islands are a true natural wonder. Witness unique wildlife, such as giant tortoises, marine iguanas, and blue-footed boobies, and snorkel among vibrant coral reefs.

2. Historic Center of Quito: Quito's Old Town, a UNESCO World Heritage site, is a treasure trove of colonial architecture, cobblestone streets, and ornate churches. Explore the iconic Plaza de la Independencia, visit the breathtaking La Compañía de Jesús Church, and admire panoramic views from El Panecillo.

3. Avenue of the Volcanoes: Stretching along the Andean highlands, the Avenue of the Volcanoes offers a breathtaking panorama of majestic volcanic peaks. Cotopaxi, Chimborazo, and

Tungurahua are just a few of the towering volcanoes that dominate the landscape, creating a photographer's paradise.

4. Amazon Rainforest: Ecuador is home to a portion of the incredible Amazon Rainforest. Embark on a jungle adventure, hike through lush foliage, and encounter exotic wildlife, including monkeys, colorful birds, and elusive jaguars.

5. Otavalo Market: Located in the town of Otavalo, this vibrant market is renowned for its indigenous crafts and textiles. Explore the stalls filled with intricately woven textiles, handcrafted jewelry, and traditional artwork while immersing yourself in the indigenous culture.

3 Days Ecuador Itinerary

This three-day itinerary offers a taste of Ecuador's diverse landscapes, rich culture, and unique experiences. From the bustling city streets of Quito to the natural wonders of the Andean highlands and the magical cloud forest, you'll create lasting memories of this remarkable country.

¶ Day 1: Quito City Tour and Old Town Exploration

Start your Ecuadorian adventure in the capital city of Quito. Begin the day by exploring the historic center, a UNESCO World Heritage site. Visit the iconic Plaza de la Independencia, admire the stunning La Compañía de Jesús Church, and take in panoramic views from El Panecillo. Immerse yourself in the vibrant atmosphere of the city's bustling streets and colorful markets. In the afternoon, head to the TelefériQo, a cable car that takes you up to the slopes of Pichincha Volcano, offering breathtaking views of Quito and its surrounding mountains. End the day with a delicious dinner, sampling traditional Ecuadorian cuisine.

¶Day 2: Otavalo Market and Andean Highlands

Wake up early and embark on a scenic drive to the town of Otavalo, known for its famous indigenous market. Explore the colorful stalls filled with handmade textiles, crafts, and traditional artwork. Engage with local artisans and learn about their weaving techniques. After shopping, venture to the nearby Peguche Waterfall for a refreshing hike through lush greenery. In the afternoon, continue your journey to the Avenue of the Volcanoes, where you can marvel at the majestic peaks of Cotopaxi, Chimborazo, and other volcanoes that dot the Andean landscape. Capture stunning photos and soak in the beauty of these natural wonders. Spend the night in a cozy hacienda, surrounded by breathtaking views of the highlands.

¶*Day 3: Mindo Cloud Forest and Chocolate Experience*
On the final day, head to the enchanting Mindo Cloud Forest, a haven of biodiversity. Embark on a thrilling zip-line adventure, explore nature trails, and spot a variety of bird species. Visit a local chocolate factory and learn about the process of making organic chocolate from the cacao bean to the final product. Participate in a hands-on chocolate-making workshop and savor the rich flavors. In the afternoon, take a leisurely hike to the mesmerizing waterfalls of Mindo, where you can cool off with a swim in pristine pools. Enjoy a relaxing picnic surrounded by the sounds of nature before returning to Quito.

7 Days Ecuador Itinerary

This seven-day itinerary offers a well-rounded experience of Ecuador's diverse landscapes, cultural heritage, and unique ecosystems. From the vibrant city life of Quito to the pristine beauty of the Galapagos Islands, Amazon Rainforest, and Andean highlands, you'll create unforgettable memories of this remarkable country.

Day 1: Quito City Tour and Old Town Exploration

Start your Ecuadorian adventure in the vibrant capital city of Quito. Spend the day exploring the historic center, a UNESCO World Heritage site. Visit the iconic Plaza de la Independencia, admire the stunning La Compañía de Jesús Church, and take in panoramic views from El Panecillo. Immerse yourself in the city's bustling streets, vibrant markets, and rich cultural heritage.

Day 2: Galapagos Islands Exploration

Fly to the Galapagos Islands and embark on a memorable exploration of this unique archipelago. Spend the day visiting various islands, each with its distinct ecosystem and wildlife. Witness giant tortoises in their natural habitat, snorkel with sea lions and colorful fish, and observe the famous Galapagos finches. Immerse yourself in the wonders of evolution and the pristine beauty of this UNESCO World Heritage site.

Day 3: Amazon Rainforest Adventure

Fly to the Amazon Rainforest, one of the most biodiverse regions on the planet. Explore the lush jungle, hike nature trails, and discover the incredible plant and animal species that call this region home. Interact with indigenous communities, learn about their traditions and sustainable practices, and embark on thrilling wildlife spotting excursions.

Day 4: Baños and Adventure Activities
Travel to the charming town of Baños, nestled in the Andean highlands. Experience adrenaline-pumping adventure activities such as zip-lining, canyoning, or biking down the scenic route of the Waterfalls Route. Soak in the relaxing thermal baths for a rejuvenating experience. Enjoy the stunning views of Tungurahua Volcano, which looms over the town.

Day 5: Avenue of the Volcanoes and Cotopaxi National Park
Embark on a scenic drive along the Avenue of the Volcanoes, passing through breathtaking landscapes. Visit Cotopaxi National Park, home to the magnificent Cotopaxi Volcano. Hike through the paramo ecosystem, enjoy the stunning views, and learn about the park's unique flora and fauna. Spend the night in a cozy mountain lodge.

Day 6: Quilotoa Lagoon and Indigenous Communities
Visit the stunning Quilotoa Lagoon, a picturesque crater lake surrounded by towering cliffs. Take a scenic hike around the rim of the crater, enjoying the panoramic views. Visit nearby indigenous communities, interact with the locals, and learn about their traditional way of life.

Day 7: Mindo Cloud Forest and Chocolate Experience
Head to the magical Mindo Cloud Forest, famous for its incredible biodiversity. Embark on nature hikes, birdwatching tours, and zip-lining adventures. Visit a local chocolate factory and participate in a hands-on chocolate-making workshop. End your journey with a relaxing picnic surrounded by the beauty of the cloud forest.

5 Low-cost Hotel Options

These low-cost hotel options in Ecuador provide travelers with comfortable accommodations at affordable prices, allowing them to make the most of their budget while exploring the country's diverse landscapes and cultural attractions.

1. **Hostal La Ronda (Quito):** Located in the heart of Quito's historic center, Hostal La Ronda offers affordable accommodation without compromising on comfort. The cozy rooms are well-maintained, and the friendly staff provides excellent service. The hostel's central location allows easy access to Quito's major attractions.

2. **Hostal Fevilamir (Cuenca):** Situated in the charming city of Cuenca, Hostal Fevilamir offers

budget-friendly rooms with basic amenities. The hostel features a communal kitchen, a rooftop terrace with panoramic city views, and a helpful front desk staff who can assist with travel arrangements and sightseeing recommendations.

3. **La Posada del Sueco (Baños):** La Posada del Sueco is a budget hotel located in the adventure town of Baños. The hotel offers comfortable rooms with private bathrooms and a complimentary breakfast. It also features a communal kitchen, a cozy lounge area, and a garden where guests can relax.

4. **Hostal Los Yutzos (Puerto Ayora, Galapagos Islands):** For those traveling to the Galapagos Islands on a budget, Hostal Los Yutzos in Puerto Ayora provides affordable accommodation. The hotel offers simple, clean rooms with private bathrooms and a convenient location near the waterfront and local attractions.

5. **La Casa del Sueno (Montañita):** Situated in the vibrant beach town of Montañita, La Casa del Sueno offers budget-friendly accommodations just a short walk from the beach. The hostel features colorful rooms, a communal kitchen, and

a lively bar area where guests can socialize and enjoy live music.

5 Luxurious Places to Stay in Ecuador

These luxurious places to stay in Ecuador provide discerning travelers with opulent accommodations, world-class amenities, and exceptional service. Whether it's immersing in the natural beauty of the Galapagos Islands, indulging in a spa retreat, or exploring Ecuador's cultural heritage, these luxurious properties offer an unforgettable experience for those seeking the ultimate in comfort and elegance.

1. *Mashpi Lodge (Mindo Cloud Forest):* Nestled in the pristine Mindo Cloud Forest, Mashpi Lodge offers a luxurious and immersive experience in the heart of nature. The eco-friendly lodge features beautifully designed rooms with panoramic views, gourmet dining, a spa, and a range of guided activities such as hiking, birdwatching, and exploring the forest canopy.

2. *Finch Bay Galapagos Hotel (Santa Cruz Island, Galapagos Islands)*: Located on Santa Cruz

Island, Finch Bay Galapagos Hotel provides an exquisite stay in the Galapagos. The hotel offers spacious rooms, a stunning pool, gourmet cuisine, and direct access to the beach. Guests can partake in wildlife excursions, snorkeling, and kayaking adventures.

3. *Hacienda Zuleta (Imbabura Province):* Hacienda Zuleta is a historic and luxurious hacienda nestled in the Andean highlands. The property features elegantly decorated rooms, a gourmet restaurant serving traditional Ecuadorian cuisine, horseback riding, hiking trails, and a working farm where guests can engage in agricultural activities.

4. *Casa Gangotena (Quito):* Situated in Quito's historic center, Casa Gangotena is a boutique hotel housed in a beautifully restored mansion. The rooms exude elegance and luxury, and the hotel features a gourmet restaurant, a rooftop terrace with panoramic city views, and a spa. Guests can explore the city's attractions, visit nearby museums, and enjoy the hotel's impeccable service.

5. *Pikaia Lodge (Santa Cruz Island, Galapagos Islands):* Pikaia Lodge offers a unique and

luxurious experience on Santa Cruz Island in the Galapagos. The lodge features spacious and contemporary rooms, a gourmet restaurant, a stunning infinity pool, and a private yacht for exploring the surrounding islands. Guests can enjoy guided wildlife encounters, snorkeling, and relaxing spa treatments.

CHAPTER 4: WHAT TO DO BEFORE TRAVELING TO ECUADOR

Before traveling to Ecuador, there are a few important things to consider and prepare for to ensure a smooth and enjoyable trip. Here are some essential steps to take before embarking on your Ecuadorian adventure:

Research and plan your itinerary: Ecuador offers a diverse range of attractions and activities, so it's important to research and plan your itinerary in advance. Decide on the regions you want to visit, such as the Galapagos Islands, the Amazon Rainforest, or the Andean highlands, and make a list of the must-see places and experiences.

Check visa requirements: Depending on your nationality, you may need a visa to enter Ecuador. Check the visa requirements well in advance and ensure you have all the necessary documentation for a smooth entry into the country.

Get travel insurance: It's always advisable to have travel insurance that covers medical expenses, trip cancellations, and other unforeseen circumstances. Make sure your insurance policy includes coverage for activities and regions you plan to visit in Ecuador.

Consult a healthcare professional: Before traveling, consult with your healthcare professional to get updated on any necessary vaccinations or medications recommended for Ecuador. This may include vaccinations for diseases such as yellow fever or typhoid.

Pack appropriately: Ecuador's diverse climate and geography mean that packing the right clothing and gear is essential. Pack layers to accommodate varying temperatures, comfortable walking shoes, insect repellent, and any specific equipment you may need for activities like hiking or snorkeling.

Learn some basic Spanish: While it's possible to get by with English in tourist areas, knowing some basic Spanish phrases can be helpful for communication and interacting with locals.

Entry Requirement

To enter Ecuador, there are certain entry requirements that travelers need to fulfill. Here are the key points to keep in mind:

Passport: All visitors to Ecuador must have a valid passport with at least six months of validity remaining from the date of entry. Ensure your passport is in good condition and has enough blank pages for immigration stamps.

Visa requirements: Depending on your nationality, you may or may not require a visa to enter Ecuador. Citizens from many countries, including the United States, Canada, the United Kingdom, Australia, and most European countries, can enter Ecuador as tourists for up to 90 days without a visa. However, it's important to check the specific visa requirements based on your citizenship before traveling.

Tourist Card: Upon arrival in Ecuador, most visitors will receive a tourist card, also known as a Tarjeta Andina de Migración (TAM). This card will be provided by the airline or at immigration. Keep the tourist card safe, as you will need to present it when leaving the country.

Return or onward ticket: Immigration may ask for proof of your return or onward travel plans, so it's advisable to have a copy of your itinerary or a return ticket.

Yellow Fever Vaccination: Travelers coming from certain countries with a risk of yellow fever transmission are required to show proof of yellow fever vaccination. Check if this requirement applies to you based on your country of origin or recent travel history.

Travel Insurance and Safety Tips

When planning a trip to Ecuador, it's crucial to prioritize your safety and well-being. Here are some travel insurance and safety tips to consider before your journey:

Travel Insurance: It's highly recommended to purchase comprehensive travel insurance that covers medical emergencies, trip cancellations or interruptions, and theft or loss of personal belongings. Ensure that your insurance policy includes coverage for activities you plan to engage in, such as adventure sports or hiking in remote areas.

Health and Safety Precautions: Consult a healthcare professional before traveling to Ecuador to get updated on any necessary vaccinations or medications. Practice good hygiene, including regular handwashing, and drink bottled or purified water. Be cautious of street food and ensure it's prepared in hygienic conditions.

Safety in Public Spaces: Exercise caution in crowded areas and be aware of your surroundings, especially in tourist hotspots where pickpocketing can occur. Keep your valuables secure and avoid displaying signs of wealth.

Transportation Safety: Use licensed and reputable transportation services. When using taxis, choose authorized and metered taxis or use reputable ride-hailing apps. If possible, avoid traveling alone at night and always inform someone of your travel plans.

Natural Hazards: Ecuador is prone to natural hazards such as earthquakes and volcanic activity. Stay informed about potential risks, follow the guidance of local authorities, and be prepared with an emergency plan.

Respect Local Customs and Culture: Familiarize yourself with Ecuadorian customs and cultural norms to show respect to the local population. Dress appropriately, particularly when visiting religious or indigenous sites.

Safety and Health Tips

When traveling to Ecuador, it's important to prioritize your safety and well-being. Here are some safety and health tips to ensure a smooth and enjoyable trip:

Stay Aware of Your Surroundings: Like any other destination, it's important to stay vigilant and aware of your surroundings. Keep an eye on your belongings, especially in crowded areas or tourist spots, and avoid displaying signs of wealth. Be cautious of pickpocketing and take necessary precautions to protect your personal belongings.

Transportation Safety: When using public transportation, choose licensed and reputable services. Use authorized taxis or reputable ride-hailing apps, and if possible, agree on the fare before starting your journey. Avoid traveling alone at night, and be cautious of unofficial taxis.

Health Precautions: Before traveling to Ecuador, consult with a healthcare professional to ensure you are up to date on routine vaccinations. Depending on your travel plans and activities, additional vaccinations may be recommended. It's also advisable to pack a basic first aid kit with essentials such as band-aids, antiseptic, and any necessary medications.

Hygiene and Food Safety: Practice good hygiene by regularly washing your hands, especially before meals. Drink bottled or purified water, and avoid consuming raw or uncooked food, including street food, to reduce the risk of foodborne illnesses.

Altitude Sickness: If you plan to visit high-altitude regions in Ecuador, such as Quito or the Andean highlands, be aware of the potential for altitude sickness. Take it easy upon arrival, stay hydrated, and give yourself time to acclimate to the altitude. If symptoms persist or worsen, seek medical attention.

Natural Hazards: Ecuador is prone to natural hazards such as earthquakes and volcanic activity. Familiarize yourself with emergency procedures and follow the guidance of local authorities. Stay informed about any potential risks and have a plan in place in case of an emergency.

Cash at the Airport is Expensive

It's important to be aware that exchanging currency or withdrawing cash at the airport can be more expensive compared to other options. Here are a few reasons why cash at the airport may come with higher costs:

- Exchange Rates: Currency exchange rates at airports tend to be less favorable compared to banks, local exchange offices, or ATMs in the city. Airport exchange services often charge higher commissions or fees, resulting in a less favorable exchange rate for travelers.

- Additional Fees: In addition to less favorable exchange rates, airport currency exchange services may charge additional fees or commissions on top of the exchange rate. These fees can further reduce the value of the currency you receive.

- Limited Options: Airports typically have limited currency exchange providers, which can create a lack of competition and give the exchange services more control over the rates they offer. With fewer options available, travelers may have little choice but to accept the higher rates.

To avoid the higher costs associated with exchanging currency at the airport, consider the following alternatives:

- Use ATMs: ATMs in Ecuador offer competitive exchange rates and often have lower fees compared to airport currency exchange services. Check with your bank before traveling to ensure your card will work internationally and to understand any associated fees.

- Exchange Currency in the City: Local banks or authorized exchange offices in major cities in Ecuador tend to offer more favorable rates compared to airport services. Take some time to research and compare rates before making your exchange.

DOs and DON'Ts in Ecuador

By following these DOs and DON'Ts, you can have a memorable and respectful experience while exploring the wonders of Ecuador. Show appreciation for the country's natural and cultural heritage, and embrace the warmth and hospitality of its people.

DOs:

■ Do explore Ecuador's diverse landscapes: From the Galapagos Islands to the Amazon Rainforest and the Andean highlands, Ecuador offers a wealth of natural wonders. Take the time to explore and appreciate the country's diverse landscapes.

■ Do try the local cuisine: Ecuadorian cuisine is rich in flavor and offers a variety of traditional dishes. Don't miss out on trying favorites like ceviche, llapingachos (potato pancakes), and seco de chivo (braised goat stew).

■ Do interact with the locals: Ecuadorians are known for their warm and friendly hospitality. Take the opportunity to engage with the locals, learn about their culture, and practice some basic Spanish phrases.

■ Do carry small change: It's always helpful to carry small denominations of local currency for small purchases, tipping, or using public transportation.

■ Do dress appropriately: Respect the local customs and dress modestly, especially when visiting churches or indigenous communities. Pack layers to accommodate varying climates and be prepared for both warm and cool temperatures.

DON'Ts:

✗ Don't drink tap water: It's advisable to stick to bottled water or purified water during your stay in Ecuador to avoid any potential health issues.

✗ Don't display excessive wealth: Avoid wearing expensive jewelry or flaunting large amounts of cash in public. This helps prevent becoming a target for theft or pickpocketing.

✗ Don't litter: Ecuador places a strong emphasis on environmental conservation. Always dispose of trash properly and respect the natural beauty of the country.

✗ Don't ignore safety precautions: Be cautious when walking in crowded areas and take necessary precautions to safeguard your belongings. Stay informed about potential safety risks, especially in unfamiliar areas or during late hours.

✗ Don't disrespect sacred sites: When visiting churches, indigenous communities, or cultural sites, be respectful of local customs and traditions. Observe any rules or guidelines and seek permission before taking photographs.

CHAPTER 5: TOP 10 MUST-TRY BEST CUISINE IN ECUADOR

Ecuador is a culinary delight, offering a diverse range of flavors and dishes influenced by its rich indigenous heritage and regional ingredients. Here are the top 10 must-try cuisines in Ecuador:

1. Ceviche: A popular coastal dish made with fresh seafood marinated in lime or bitter orange juice, served with onions, tomatoes, and cilantro.

2. Llapingachos: Delicious potato pancakes typically stuffed with cheese and served with a variety of accompaniments like fried eggs, avocado, and chorizo.

3. Seco de Chivo: A hearty stew made with tender goat meat, cooked slowly with beer, herbs, and spices. It's usually served with rice, avocado, and fried plantains.

4. Locro de Papa: A comforting potato and cheese soup with chunks of avocado and served with toasted corn kernels.

5. Hornado: A traditional dish of roasted pork, marinated with garlic and spices, served with potatoes, mote (hominy), and llapingachos.

6. Cuy: Guinea pig is a delicacy in Ecuador and is often roasted or fried. It's a must-try for the adventurous food lover.

7. Encebollado: A popular coastal soup made with fresh tuna, yuca, onions, tomatoes, and cilantro. It's often enjoyed for breakfast or as a hangover cure.

8. Fanesca: A traditional Easter soup made with 12 different grains and beans, accompanied by salted codfish, cheese, and empanadas.

9. Empanadas de Viento: Crispy, deep-fried pastries filled with cheese and topped with powdered sugar. They are a popular snack or street food option.

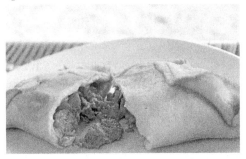

10. Choclo con Queso: Grilled corn on the cob served with fresh cheese, often enjoyed as a snack or side dish.

Currency and Exchange Tips

When traveling to Ecuador, it's important to be aware of the currency used and understand how to handle exchanges. Here are some currency and exchange tips to keep in mind:

° Currency: The official currency of Ecuador is the US Dollar (USD). It's advisable to carry small denominations and a mix of bills to facilitate transactions.

° Exchange Rates: Stay informed about the current exchange rates to ensure you get a fair deal when exchanging currency. Banks and authorized exchange offices generally offer competitive rates.

° Exchange Options: It's recommended to exchange currency at banks or authorized exchange offices for better rates and security. Avoid exchanging money on the street or with unauthorized individuals, as this can lead to scams or counterfeit bills.

° ATM Withdrawals: ATMs are widely available in major cities and tourist areas. Use ATMs associated with reputable banks and be mindful of any associated fees charged by your bank for international withdrawals.

° Credit Cards: Major credit cards such as Visa and Mastercard are widely accepted in hotels, restaurants, and larger establishments. However, it's always a good idea to carry some cash for smaller vendors or in case of technical issues with card machines.

° Notify Your Bank: Before traveling to Ecuador, inform your bank about your travel plans to avoid any issues with using your cards. This prevents your transactions from being flagged as suspicious and potentially declined.

° Keep Receipts: When exchanging currency or making transactions, retain your receipts. These may be required for future exchanges or proof of purchase.

° Check for Counterfeit Bills: Familiarize yourself with Ecuadorian currency to recognize security features and avoid accepting counterfeit bills. Pay attention to watermarks, security threads, and other identifying marks.

Tipping in Ecuador

Tipping customs in Ecuador are similar to those in many other countries. While tipping is not mandatory, it's customary to show appreciation for good service. Here are some guidelines for tipping in Ecuador:

- Restaurants: In restaurants, it's common to leave a tip of around 10% of the total bill if a service charge has not already been included. Check the bill to see if a service charge has been added, and if not, leave a cash tip on the table for the server.

- Bars: When ordering drinks at a bar, it's customary to leave a small tip, usually a dollar or two per round or as a percentage of the total bill.

- Hotels: Tipping hotel staff is a common practice in Ecuador. For hotel housekeeping, leaving a few dollars per day is appreciated. Bellhops or porters can be tipped a couple of dollars for their assistance.

- Tour Guides and Drivers: If you take a guided tour or use the services of a driver, it's customary to tip them as a token of appreciation. The amount can vary depending on the length of the tour or the level of service provided.

- Other Services: In other service industries, such as spa treatments or hair salons, a tip of around 10% is customary if you're satisfied with the service.

Remember, tipping is discretionary, and the amount can vary based on your satisfaction with the service received. It's always a good idea to have small bills or coins on hand for tipping, as larger denominations may not be practical.

Local Custom and Etiquette

When visiting Ecuador, it's important to be aware of the local customs and etiquette to show respect for the country's culture and traditions. Here are some key points to keep in mind:

Greetings: Ecuadorians are warm and friendly people. It's customary to greet others with a handshake, and close friends and family may exchange kisses on the cheek. Use formal titles like "Señor" (Mr.) or "Señora" (Mrs.) when addressing someone you've just met.

Personal Space: Ecuadorians tend to stand closer during conversations compared to people from some other cultures. Respect personal space but be prepared for a closer proximity when engaging in conversations.

Politeness: Courtesy is highly valued in Ecuadorian culture. Use "por favor" (please) and "gracias" (thank you) in your interactions. It's also customary to address elders or authority figures with respect.

Punctuality: While being on time is appreciated, Ecuador operates on "Ecuadorian time," which can be more relaxed. Allow for some flexibility in schedules and be patient if appointments or events start a bit later than planned.

Dress Code: Dress modestly and respectfully, especially when visiting churches, indigenous communities, or rural areas. Avoid wearing revealing or provocative clothing in public places.

Gift Giving: When invited to someone's home, it's customary to bring a small gift, such as flowers, chocolates, or a bottle of wine. Gifts should be given and received with both hands, and it's polite to open gifts received in front of the giver.

Dining Etiquette: Wait for the host or elder to start eating before you begin. Keep your hands visible on the table, and it's considered polite to finish everything on your plate.

Fresh fruits at Andean market, Otavalo, Ecuador

CHAPTER 6: TIPS AND CONSIDERATION

When traveling to Ecuador, there are a few tips and considerations that can help ensure a smooth and enjoyable experience. Here are some important points to keep in mind:

Language: The official language of Ecuador is Spanish. While some locals may speak English, especially in tourist areas, it's helpful to learn a few basic Spanish phrases to facilitate communication.

Bargaining: Bargaining is common in local markets and street vendors. Feel free to negotiate prices, but do so respectfully and with a friendly demeanor.

Altitude: Ecuador has diverse landscapes, including high-altitude regions like the Andean Highlands. If you plan to visit such areas, take precautions for altitude sickness by staying hydrated, avoiding strenuous activities initially, and acclimatizing gradually.

Respect for Indigenous Communities: Ecuador is home to various indigenous communities with rich cultural traditions. When visiting these communities, respect their customs, seek permission before taking photographs, and purchase handicrafts directly from artisans.

Environmental Responsibility: Ecuador is known for its exceptional biodiversity and natural beauty. Practice responsible tourism by following designated trails, avoiding littering, and respecting wildlife and natural habitats.

Health and Safety: Ensure you have travel insurance that covers medical expenses in case of emergencies. It's also advisable to check for any required vaccinations before your trip and to take precautions against mosquito-borne diseases in certain areas.

Electricity: Ecuador operates on 110-120 volts, with outlets accepting two- or three-pronged plugs. Bring a universal adapter if your devices use different voltage or plug types.

Visiting Ecuador on a Budget

I had always dreamed of exploring this beautiful country, but my budget had limited my travel options in the past. Determined to make the most of my adventure without breaking the bank, I embarked on a journey to experience Ecuador on a budget.

My first task was finding affordable accommodation. I discovered cozy hostels nestled in the heart of bustling cities and serene guesthouses tucked away in picturesque towns. These budget-friendly options not only provided a comfortable place to rest my head but also introduced me to fellow travelers from around the world, sharing stories and tips along the way.

Ecuador's vibrant street food scene became my culinary playground. I savored the aroma of freshly cooked empanadas and indulged in mouthwatering ceviche from humble food carts. Local eateries offered "menu del día," providing a complete meal at a fraction of the cost. Each bite was a delightful fusion of flavors that captured the essence of Ecuador's cuisine.

Navigating the country was a breeze with the extensive network of buses. I hopped on colorful vehicles, traversing the diverse landscapes of Ecuador. From the towering peaks of the Andes to the lush jungles of the Amazon, I marveled at the breathtaking beauty that surrounded me, all while keeping my transportation expenses minimal.

Ecuador's natural wonders provided endless adventures without straining my wallet. I trekked through misty cloud forests, swam in crystal-clear lagoons, and marveled at cascading waterfalls. The country's national parks and reserves offered an abundance of hiking trails and wildlife encounters, allowing me to immerse myself in the splendor of nature.

Engaging with the local culture became a highlight of my budget-friendly journey. I explored indigenous markets, bargaining for unique handicrafts and souvenirs. I joined free city walking tours led by passionate locals who shared their knowledge and anecdotes about Ecuador's rich history and culture. And when I needed a break from the bustling cities, I volunteered with community projects, exchanging my time and skills for meaningful experiences and connections.

Visiting Ecuador on a budget had not only allowed me to witness its natural wonders but also to connect with its people and immerse myself in the vibrant tapestry of its culture. With careful planning, an open mind, and a spirit of adventure, I had discovered that exploring Ecuador on a budget was not only possible but also a rewarding and unforgettable experience.

Navigating Ecuador: Public Transportation and Getting Around the Country

As I embarked on my journey through Ecuador, I quickly realized that the country had a well-established public transportation system that made getting around a breeze. From bustling cities to remote villages, here's how I navigated Ecuador's diverse landscapes:

Buses became my trusty companions. They formed the backbone of Ecuador's transportation network, connecting cities, towns, and even rural areas. I hopped on colorful buses, each with its own unique character, and embarked on scenic journeys. The fares were affordable, making it an excellent option for budget-conscious travelers like me. I found bus terminals in major cities, where I could easily purchase tickets for my desired destination.

For shorter distances within cities, taxis were a convenient mode of transportation. I made sure to use licensed taxis with meters or agreed upon a fare before getting in. Ride-hailing apps also provided a reliable and safe option, especially in larger urban areas.

In some areas, like the Galapagos Islands, water taxis or small boats served as the primary means of transportation between islands or to reach remote spots.

These aquatic adventures added an extra touch of excitement to my travels.

When exploring more remote regions, like the Amazon rainforest or the highlands, I opted for guided tours or hired private transportation services. These options ensured that I could access off-the-beaten-path destinations and enjoy personalized experiences tailored to my interests.

Navigating Ecuador's cities was made easier by the presence of pedestrian-friendly streets and bike lanes. In cities like Quito and Cuenca, I rented bicycles to explore at my own pace, taking in the sights and sounds while enjoying the freedom of two wheels.

Accommodation Options: Hotels, Resorts, and Homestays in Ecuador

When it comes to finding a place to stay in Ecuador, travelers are spoilt for choice with a range of accommodation options catering to different preferences and budgets. Whether you're seeking luxury, comfort, or an immersive cultural experience, Ecuador has it all.

Hotels in Ecuador vary from boutique establishments to well-known international chains, offering a wide range of amenities and services. From cozy rooms with local charm to upscale suites with breathtaking views, hotels cater to the needs of all types of travelers. Many hotels also feature on-site restaurants, swimming pools, and spa facilities, ensuring a relaxing and convenient stay.

For those seeking a luxurious escape, Ecuador boasts stunning resorts nestled in picturesque locations. These resorts offer world-class amenities such as private beaches, infinity pools, gourmet dining, and indulgent spa treatments. Immerse yourself in the lap of luxury and let the natural beauty of Ecuador surround you.

For a more immersive cultural experience, consider staying in a homestay. Homestays allow you to live with local families, providing a glimpse into the daily lives, customs, and traditions of the Ecuadorian people. You'll have the opportunity to interact with your hosts, share meals, and learn about the local way of life. Homestays offer a unique and enriching experience, fostering cultural exchange and creating lifelong memories.

In addition to hotels, resorts, and homestays, Ecuador also offers eco-lodges and hostels for budget-conscious travelers. Eco-lodges blend harmoniously with the natural surroundings, providing a sustainable and eco-friendly accommodation option. Hostels, on the other hand, offer affordable dormitory-style rooms and communal spaces where travelers can connect with like-minded individuals.

What to Pack For Your Trip to Ecuador

As you prepare for your adventure in Ecuador, it's important to pack wisely to ensure a comfortable and enjoyable journey. Here are some essential items to consider including in your packing list:

Layered Clothing: Ecuador's climate varies greatly depending on the region and altitude. Pack a variety of clothing options, including lightweight and breathable clothes for warmer areas, as well as warmer layers for cooler regions like the highlands. Don't forget a rain jacket or poncho, as showers can occur unexpectedly.

Comfortable Footwear: Ecuador's diverse terrain calls for comfortable walking shoes or hiking boots, especially if you plan to explore the mountains, forests, or volcanic landscapes. Sandals or flip-flops are ideal for beach areas.

Travel Documents: Carry your passport, travel insurance information, and any necessary visas or permits. Make copies of these documents and keep them in a separate place.

Sun Protection: Ecuador's proximity to the equator means strong sun exposure. Pack sunscreen, a wide-brimmed hat, sunglasses, and lightweight long-sleeved shirts to protect your skin from the sun's rays.

Insect Repellent: Some regions in Ecuador, particularly the Amazon rainforest, are prone to mosquitos and other insects. Pack insect repellent with a high concentration of DEET or a natural alternative.

Medications and First Aid Kit: If you take any prescription medications, be sure to bring an adequate supply. Additionally, pack a basic first aid kit with essentials such as band-aids, antiseptic cream, and any specific medications you may need (e.g., for altitude sickness).

Adapter and Charger: Ecuador's electrical outlets typically use 120 volts, so bring a universal adapter and charger for your electronic devices.

Nightlife in Ecuador

When the sun sets in Ecuador, a vibrant and lively nightlife scene comes alive, offering a range of entertainment options to suit different tastes and preferences. Whether you're a party animal or seeking a more relaxed evening, Ecuador has something for everyone.

Major cities like Quito and Guayaquil boast a buzzing nightlife, with an array of bars, clubs, and live music venues. In these urban hubs, you'll find trendy bars serving up craft cocktails, local beers, and a variety of spirits. Dance the night away to Latin rhythms like salsa, merengue, and reggaeton in energetic clubs where locals and tourists come together for a memorable night out.

In coastal cities like Montañita and Salinas, beachfront clubs and bars create a lively atmosphere. Enjoy beach parties, live music, and fire shows as you sip on tropical cocktails and dance barefoot in the sand. The coastal nightlife in Ecuador offers a relaxed and carefree vibe, perfect for those seeking a beachside fiesta.

For a more laid-back evening, explore the quaint towns and villages where you'll find cozy pubs, jazz clubs, and rooftop terraces offering stunning views. Enjoy live music performances ranging from traditional Andean music to jazz and blues.

It's worth mentioning that Ecuador's nightlife scene caters to all budgets. You'll find upscale nightclubs with

VIP sections and exclusive experiences, as well as budget-friendly bars and venues that offer affordable drinks and entertainment.

It's important to exercise caution and be aware of your surroundings when enjoying the nightlife in Ecuador, just as you would in any other destination. Stick to well-lit and crowded areas, travel in groups, and take necessary precautions to ensure a safe and enjoyable night out.

Shopping in Ecuador

Ecuador offers a unique and diverse shopping experience, with a variety of goods and crafts that reflect the country's rich culture and traditions. From bustling markets to upscale boutiques, here's what you can expect when it comes to shopping in Ecuador.

One of the highlights of shopping in Ecuador is exploring the vibrant local markets. These markets are a treasure trove of handicrafts, textiles, and artwork. Otavalo Market, located in the Andean region, is renowned for its colorful textiles, handmade crafts, and traditional clothing. Here, you can find beautifully woven tapestries, alpaca wool products, and intricately embroidered garments.

In the capital city of Quito, the Old Town area is home to many artisanal shops and galleries. Here, you can find unique ceramics, jewelry, and traditional Ecuadorian crafts. The city's modern shopping centers also offer a wide range of international and local brands.

If you're a fan of vibrant and exquisite Panama hats, a visit to Montecristi is a must. Known as the birthplace of the Panama hat, this small town produces some of the finest and most sought-after hats in the world. You can witness the intricate hat-making process and purchase an authentic piece to take home.

Ecuador is also famous for its cacao production, making it an ideal destination for chocolate lovers. Explore chocolate shops and factories, and indulge in high-quality, locally-made chocolate bars and truffles.

When it comes to souvenirs, keep an eye out for traditional artwork, indigenous crafts, and handmade jewelry. These unique items make for meaningful and memorable keepsakes from your Ecuadorian adventure.

Remember to brush up on your bargaining skills, as haggling is common in markets and small shops. It's also important to be aware of the regulations regarding the export of certain goods, particularly if you plan to bring back animal products or plant-based items.

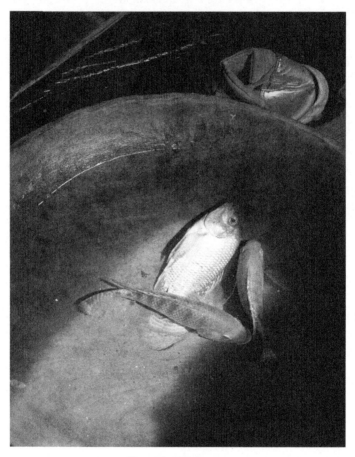

Ecuador Fish

CHAPTER 7: INSIDER TIPS FOR EXPLORING ECUADOR

When it comes to exploring Ecuador, having some insider tips can greatly enhance your experience and make your journey even more enjoyable. From cultural insights to practical advice, here are some valuable tips to keep in mind as you embark on your Ecuadorian adventure:

Embrace the Diversity: Ecuador is a country of remarkable diversity, both in terms of landscapes and cultures. From the Andean highlands to the Amazon rainforest and the stunning coastline, make sure to explore different regions and immerse yourself in the unique experiences each has to offer.

Learn Some Spanish: While you can get by with English in major tourist areas, knowing a few basic Spanish phrases will go a long way in connecting with locals and navigating everyday interactions.

Try the Local Cuisine: Ecuadorian cuisine is a delightful mix of flavors and influences. Don't miss the chance to try traditional dishes like ceviche, llapingachos (potato pancakes), and locro de papas (potato soup). Be adventurous and sample street food to truly savor the local flavors.

Pack for Variable Weather: Ecuador's weather can be unpredictable, so pack layers to accommodate varying temperatures and conditions. It's not uncommon to experience different climates within a single day, so come prepared with a mix of clothing options.

Respect the Environment and Culture: Ecuador takes pride in its natural wonders and cultural heritage. Show respect for the environment by practicing responsible tourism and following guidelines for conservation. Similarly, respect the customs and traditions of the local communities you visit.

Outdoor Adventures: Hiking, Biking, and Wildlife Encounters

For adventure enthusiasts and nature lovers, Ecuador is a paradise waiting to be explored. The country's diverse landscapes, from towering mountains to lush rainforests, provide a playground for outdoor activities and thrilling experiences.

Hiking is a popular activity in Ecuador, with a multitude of trails offering breathtaking views and encounters with stunning natural wonders. The famous Quilotoa Loop takes you through remote Andean villages and leads to the mesmerizing Quilotoa crater lake. The challenging trek to the summit of Cotopaxi, one of the world's highest active volcanoes, rewards hikers with awe-inspiring vistas.

Mountain biking is another exhilarating way to experience Ecuador's stunning scenery. Ride along the slopes of the Andes, passing through picturesque valleys and vibrant highland villages. The "Avenue of the Volcanoes" offers an unforgettable biking experience, with close-up views of several towering volcanoes along the way.

Ecuador's rainforests provide the perfect setting for wildlife encounters and immersive experiences. Explore the Amazon basin, where you can embark on guided jungle hikes, canoe excursions, and even spend a night in a remote jungle lodge. Keep an eye out for diverse wildlife, including monkeys, sloths, toucans, and colorful macaws.

If you're seeking an adrenaline rush, consider white-water rafting on the Napo River or canyoning in the stunning waterfalls of Baños. For the ultimate adventure, head to the Galápagos Islands, where you can swim with sea turtles, snorkel with marine iguanas, and observe the unique wildlife that inspired Charles Darwin's theory of evolution.

Indigenous Communities and Cultural Experiences

Ecuador is a country rich in indigenous heritage, with over a dozen distinct indigenous groups. Exploring the vibrant cultures and traditions of these communities provides a unique and immersive experience for travelers.

Visiting indigenous communities in Ecuador offers a glimpse into their way of life, traditions, and ancient customs. From the colorful Otavalo market to the remote villages of the Amazon rainforest, you can witness their traditional arts, crafts, music, and rituals firsthand.

Participating in community-based tourism initiatives allows you to interact with indigenous locals and learn about their history and beliefs. You can engage in activities such as traditional weaving, pottery making, or learning about medicinal plants from local shamans.

The Inti Raymi festival, celebrated by the indigenous communities in the Andean region, is a vibrant and lively cultural event that showcases their ancient rituals and dances. Witnessing these colorful festivities is an unforgettable experience that offers a deeper understanding of their spiritual connection with nature and ancestral traditions.

Respect for indigenous cultures is paramount during these encounters. Learning a few basic phrases in their native languages and dressing modestly demonstrates appreciation for their customs.

By engaging with indigenous communities, you not only gain insight into their rich heritage but also contribute to their sustainable development and cultural preservation. It is an opportunity to foster mutual understanding and appreciation while supporting local livelihoods.

Gastronomy: Exploring Ecuadorian Cuisine

Ecuadorian cuisine is a delightful fusion of indigenous, Spanish, and Afro-Ecuadorian influences, resulting in a rich and diverse culinary tapestry. Exploring Ecuador's gastronomy is an essential part of any visit to the country, offering a tantalizing journey for your taste buds.

One of Ecuador's most famous dishes is ceviche, a refreshing seafood dish marinated in lime juice and served with onions, tomatoes, and cilantro. Each coastal region adds its own unique twist to this classic dish, making it a must-try culinary delight.

Another popular dish is the hearty and flavorful Ecuadorian soup called locro de papa. Made with potatoes, cheese, avocados, and corn, this thick and creamy soup is a comfort food that showcases the country's agricultural heritage.

Ecuador is also renowned for its wide variety of tropical fruits, such as maracuyá (passion fruit), naranjilla (a citrus-like fruit), and guanábana (soursop). These fruits are used in refreshing juices, smoothies, and desserts, adding a burst of tropical flavors to your palate.

For those seeking a unique culinary experience, try cuy (guinea pig), a traditional Andean delicacy. Roasted or fried, it is a dish that showcases the cultural traditions of the indigenous communities in the highlands.

To complement your meal, indulge in Ecuador's renowned chocolate. The country's cacao beans are highly regarded for their exceptional quality, and you can sample a wide range of delicious chocolate bars and confections made by local artisans.

Festivals and Celebrations

Ecuador is a country that loves to celebrate, and throughout the year, you'll find a colorful array of festivals and celebrations that showcase the country's vibrant culture and traditions. From ancient indigenous rituals to religious processions and lively street parties, Ecuador's festivals are a sight to behold.

One of the most iconic celebrations in Ecuador is the Inti Raymi, also known as the Festival of the Sun. Held during the summer solstice, this ancient Inca festival celebrates the sun god and is marked by colorful parades, traditional dances, and elaborate ceremonies.

During the Carnival season, you can witness lively water fights and playful street parties across the country. The cities of Guaranda and Ambato are renowned for their vibrant Carnival celebrations, featuring costumed dancers, live music, and the traditional "Mama Negra" parade.

Holy Week, leading up to Easter, is another significant time for celebrations in Ecuador. In the city of Quito, you can witness the grand procession of the "Jesus del Gran Poder," where thousands of participants dressed in traditional attire parade through the streets, reenacting biblical scenes.

The Day of the Dead, known as Día de los Difuntos, is a unique and heartfelt celebration where families gather in cemeteries to honor their departed loved ones. Graves are adorned with flowers, candles, and offerings, creating a colorful and spiritual atmosphere.

The Yamor Festival in Otavalo is a celebration of gratitude for the harvest and indigenous culture. Visitors can enjoy music, dance performances, and the traditional "Yamor Runa" parade, showcasing the vibrant traditions of the Otavalo community.

CHAPTER 8: MUST-SEE DESTINATIONS IN ECUADOR

Ecuador is a country brimming with breathtaking landscapes, rich cultural heritage, and diverse natural wonders. From the majestic Andean mountains to the lush Amazon rainforest and the captivating Galápagos Islands, there are several must-see destinations that should be on every traveler's itinerary.

Quito, the capital city, is a UNESCO World Heritage site and a treasure trove of colonial architecture. Explore the historic Old Town, visit the impressive churches, and take in panoramic views of the city from the famous El Panecillo viewpoint.

The Galápagos Islands, located in the Pacific Ocean, offer a truly unique and unparalleled experience. Discover the fascinating wildlife, including giant tortoises, marine iguanas, and blue-footed boobies, as you explore the diverse ecosystems of this renowned archipelago.

The enchanting Amazon rainforest beckons adventurers with its unparalleled biodiversity and pristine landscapes. Take a river cruise, hike through the jungle, and encounter an incredible array of wildlife, from playful monkeys to colorful birds.

For nature lovers, a visit to the Cotopaxi National Park is a must. Explore the stunning landscapes surrounding the Cotopaxi volcano, hike to breathtaking viewpoints, and spot llamas and wild horses along the way.

The historic city of Cuenca is renowned for its well-preserved colonial architecture and charming cobblestone streets. Visit its impressive cathedrals, explore the local markets, and immerse yourself in the vibrant arts and crafts scene.

Quito: Colonial Charms and Modern Delights

Quito, the capital city of Ecuador, is a captivating blend of colonial charm and modern delights. Nestled in the Andes Mountains, this UNESCO World Heritage site is a city of contrasts, where ancient history meets contemporary vibrancy.

The historic Old Town, known as the "Centro Histórico," is a treasure trove of colonial architecture and cultural landmarks. Stroll through its narrow streets, lined with beautifully preserved buildings and ornate churches. Visit the iconic Plaza de la Independencia, where you can admire the grand Presidential Palace and the impressive Metropolitan Cathedral.

One of the must-see attractions in Quito is the stunning Basílica del Voto Nacional, an awe-inspiring Gothic Revival church. Climb to the top of its towers for panoramic views of the city, or venture inside to marvel at the intricate stained glass windows and exquisite craftsmanship.

For a taste of modern Quito, head to the bustling Mariscal district. Here, you'll find a lively atmosphere with trendy cafes, eclectic shops, and vibrant nightlife. Indulge in delicious Ecuadorian cuisine at one of the many restaurants, or explore the local craft markets for unique souvenirs.

For a truly unique experience, take a ride on the Teleférico, a cable car that transports you to the summit of the Pichincha volcano. From here, you can enjoy breathtaking views of Quito and the surrounding mountains.

Galápagos Islands: Unique Wildlife and Natural Beauty

The Galápagos Islands, located in the Pacific Ocean off the coast of Ecuador, are a true natural wonder and a haven for wildlife enthusiasts. This remarkable archipelago is renowned for its unique biodiversity, captivating landscapes, and its significance in Charles Darwin's theory of evolution.

The Galápagos Islands are home to an incredible array of endemic species found nowhere else on Earth. From giant tortoises and marine iguanas to blue-footed boobies and Galápagos penguins, the islands offer a rare opportunity to witness wildlife in its natural habitat. Snorkel with playful sea lions, swim alongside graceful sea turtles, and marvel at the diverse marine life that thrives in the crystal-clear waters.

Exploring the islands, you'll encounter stunning landscapes ranging from volcanic formations to pristine white-sand beaches. Each island boasts its own distinct character and offers unique experiences. From the volcanic landscapes of Fernandina Island to the iconic Kicker Rock on San Cristobal Island, there is no shortage of natural wonders to discover.

To protect the fragile ecosystems of the Galápagos Islands, access is carefully regulated, and visitors are required to be accompanied by certified guides. This ensures that the islands' natural beauty and wildlife are preserved for future generations.

Cuenca: Cultural Heritage and Architecture

Cuenca, a picturesque city in southern Ecuador, is a UNESCO World Heritage site renowned for its rich cultural heritage and stunning colonial architecture. This charming city is nestled in the Andean highlands and offers visitors a glimpse into Ecuador's colonial past.

Walking through the streets of Cuenca is like stepping back in time. The city's historic center is a maze of cobblestone streets, lined with beautifully preserved colonial buildings, elegant churches, and picturesque plazas. The iconic blue-domed Cathedral of the Immaculate Conception, with its intricate facade, is a sight to behold.

One of the highlights of Cuenca is its vibrant arts and crafts scene. The city is famous for its skilled artisans who create exquisite ceramics, textiles, and traditional crafts. Explore the workshops and galleries in the San Blas neighborhood to admire their craftsmanship and perhaps even bring home a unique handmade souvenir.

Cuenca is also home to numerous museums and cultural institutions that showcase the region's history and artistic heritage. The Pumapungo Museum, located in an archaeological park, offers insights into the ancient cultures that once thrived in the area, while the Museum of Modern Art showcases contemporary Ecuadorian art.

In addition to its architectural and cultural treasures, Cuenca is surrounded by breathtaking natural beauty. The nearby Cajas National Park is a paradise for nature lovers, with its stunning lakes and hiking trails.

Amazon Rainforest: Biodiversity and Adventure

The Amazon Rainforest in Ecuador is a vast and biodiverse ecosystem that offers a truly immersive and adventurous experience for nature enthusiasts. Covering a significant portion of the country, the Amazon is a haven for wildlife, indigenous communities, and ecological wonders.

Exploring the Amazon Rainforest allows you to witness the incredible biodiversity that thrives within its dense vegetation. From vibrant bird species and elusive jungle cats to playful monkeys and colorful frogs, the rainforest is teeming with life. Take guided walks through the jungle, venture on canoe trips along the winding rivers, and embark on night hikes to witness the nocturnal creatures that come alive in this magical environment.

Interacting with indigenous communities is a unique opportunity to learn about their rich traditions and deep connection with the rainforest. Local guides can introduce you to their way of life, their sustainable practices, and their ancient knowledge of the plants and animals that inhabit the jungle.

For adrenaline seekers, the Amazon offers thrilling adventures such as zip-lining through the canopy, kayaking in the rivers, and even swimming with pink river dolphins. The possibilities for exploration and adventure are endless in this vast and diverse rainforest.

Otavalo: Indigenous Markets and Crafts

Located in the northern Andes of Ecuador, Otavalo is a charming town known for its vibrant indigenous culture and world-famous markets. It is a must-visit destination for those seeking authentic experiences and the opportunity to immerse themselves in the rich traditions of the local communities.

The Otavalo Market is the heart and soul of the town, attracting visitors from around the world. Here, you can wander through stalls filled with colorful textiles, intricate weavings, handmade crafts, and traditional clothing. The market is a true feast for the senses, where you can witness the craftsmanship and skill of the local artisans.

Beyond the market, Otavalo offers a glimpse into the daily lives of the indigenous communities that call this region home. Take the time to visit nearby villages, such as Peguche and Cotacachi, where you can observe traditional weaving techniques, participate in cultural ceremonies, and learn about the customs and rituals that have been passed down through generations.

The surrounding natural beauty of Otavalo is also worth exploring. Visit the stunning Cuicocha Lake, nestled within the crater of an ancient volcano, and hike the scenic trails that offer breathtaking views of the surrounding mountains and valleys.

CHAPTER 9: IMMERSING IN ECUADORIAN CULTURE

From the indigenous communities with their vibrant traditions to the colonial towns steeped in history, Ecuador offers a fascinating tapestry of cultural immersion.

One of the best ways to immerse yourself in Ecuadorian culture is by connecting with the indigenous communities that call this land home. Engage in authentic experiences such as participating in traditional ceremonies, learning about ancient agricultural practices, or witnessing the art of weaving and handicrafts firsthand. These interactions provide a unique insight into the customs, beliefs, and way of life that have been preserved for generations.

Exploring the colonial towns of Ecuador, such as Quito and Cuenca, allows you to step back in time and appreciate the rich architectural heritage left behind by the Spanish colonizers. Stroll through the cobblestone streets, marvel at the beautifully preserved churches, and visit the museums that showcase the country's history and art.

Sampling the local cuisine is another essential part of immersing in Ecuadorian culture. Indulge in traditional dishes such as ceviche, llapingachos (potato pancakes), and seco de chivo (stewed goat), and savor the flavors of Ecuadorian cuisine. You can also take part in cooking classes to learn the secrets behind preparing these delectable dishes.

Attending festivals and celebrations throughout the country offers a firsthand experience of the vibrant traditions and festivities that define Ecuadorian culture. From the vibrant colors of Inti Raymi (Sun Festival) to the solemn processions of Semana Santa (Holy Week), these events showcase the passion and spirit of the Ecuadorian people.

Indigenous Traditions and Rituals

Ecuador is home to a diverse array of indigenous communities, each with its own unique traditions and rituals that have been passed down through generations. These indigenous cultures form an integral part of Ecuador's cultural tapestry, offering a fascinating glimpse into ancient customs and beliefs.

From the Kichwa people of the Amazon rainforest to the Otavalo community in the Andean highlands, indigenous traditions are deeply rooted in the daily lives of these communities. Rituals are performed to honor nature, celebrate harvests, and mark important life milestones.

One of the most well-known indigenous rituals in Ecuador is the Inti Raymi, or Sun Festival, which takes place during the summer solstice. This celebration pays homage to the sun, an important deity in many indigenous cultures, through music, dance, and offerings. Witnessing the vibrant costumes, rhythmic dances, and spiritual ceremonies of the Inti Raymi is a mesmerizing experience.

Another significant tradition is the yachay, or shamanic practice, which is deeply ingrained in indigenous cultures. Shamans serve as spiritual guides, healers, and intermediaries between the human and spirit worlds. Participating in a traditional shamanic ceremony can offer a profound insight into the indigenous worldview and their connection with nature.

Indigenous communities also place great importance on the preservation of ancestral knowledge, particularly in practices such as weaving and pottery. These traditional crafts are not only exquisite works of art but also represent the cultural identity and heritage of the indigenous peoples.

Museums and Art Galleries

Ecuador is a treasure trove of cultural artifacts and artistic expressions, showcased in its numerous museums and art galleries. From pre-Columbian artifacts to contemporary masterpieces, these institutions provide a glimpse into the rich history and vibrant artistic scene of the country.

One of the most prominent museums in Ecuador is the Museo Nacional del Ecuador in Quito. Housed in a grand colonial building, it houses an extensive collection of archaeological artifacts, religious art, and historical exhibits that chronicle the country's past. Visitors can immerse themselves in Ecuador's rich heritage and gain a deeper understanding of its cultural evolution.

For art enthusiasts, the Museo de Arte Contemporáneo in Quito is a must-visit destination. It showcases a diverse range of contemporary works by Ecuadorian and international artists, pushing the boundaries of artistic expression. The museum hosts rotating exhibitions and offers a platform for emerging talents, providing a dynamic and ever-changing art experience.

In Cuenca, the Museo de Arte Moderno showcases the best of modern and contemporary art in Ecuador. The museum features a mix of local and international artists, highlighting the city's vibrant artistic scene. With its striking architecture and thought-provoking exhibitions, it is a hub for creativity and cultural exchange.

Throughout the country, there are also smaller art galleries and cultural centers that promote local artists and craftspeople. These spaces offer an intimate setting to appreciate paintings, sculptures, and traditional crafts, often with the opportunity to meet the artists themselves.

Traditional Crafts and Souvenirs

Ecuador is renowned for its rich tradition of craftsmanship, with artisans skillfully creating unique and intricate pieces that reflect the country's cultural diversity. Exploring traditional crafts and souvenirs in Ecuador offers an opportunity to bring home a piece of the country's heritage and support local artisans.

One of the most iconic traditional crafts in Ecuador is weaving. Indigenous communities, such as the Otavalo and Salasaka, are known for their mastery of weaving techniques. Beautifully woven textiles, including ponchos, scarves, and blankets, showcase vibrant colors and intricate patterns. These textiles are not only exquisite in design but also represent centuries-old traditions and stories.

Another popular craft in Ecuador is the creation of Panama hats, known locally as "sombreros de paja toquilla." Despite their name, these finely woven hats are actually of Ecuadorian origin. Crafted from the fibers of the toquilla palm, they are meticulously woven into lightweight and flexible hats. Purchasing an authentic Panama hat in Ecuador allows visitors to bring home a piece of Ecuadorian craftsmanship and style.

Wood carving is another traditional craft deeply rooted in Ecuadorian culture. Intricate sculptures depicting indigenous figures, animals, and mythical creatures showcase the craftsmanship and artistic skills of the artisans. From small trinkets to larger sculptures, these wooden pieces make for unique and meaningful souvenirs.

Other traditional crafts in Ecuador include pottery, silverwork, and jewelry-making. From intricately painted ceramics to finely crafted silver earrings and necklaces, these crafts highlight the skill and creativity of Ecuadorian artisans.

CHAPTER 10: UNDERSTANDING FOREIGN TRANSACTION FEES

When traveling to Ecuador, it's essential to be aware of foreign transaction fees to avoid any unexpected charges and manage your expenses effectively. Foreign transaction fees are fees imposed by banks or credit card companies for using your card in a foreign currency or making purchases abroad. Here's what you need to know:

Credit Cards: Before using your credit card in Ecuador, check with your bank or credit card company to understand their foreign transaction fee policy. Some credit cards charge a percentage fee on every transaction made in a foreign currency, while others may have no foreign transaction fees at all. It's advisable to opt for a card with no or minimal foreign transaction fees to save on unnecessary expenses.

ATM Withdrawals: When using ATMs in Ecuador, you may encounter fees from both your home bank and the local bank. Your home bank may charge a foreign transaction fee for withdrawing cash in a foreign currency, while the local bank may charge an additional ATM fee. To minimize these fees, consider withdrawing larger amounts of cash at once instead of making multiple small withdrawals.

Currency Exchange: When exchanging currency in Ecuador, be aware of the exchange rates and any associated fees. It's recommended to exchange money at authorized exchange offices or banks to ensure fair rates and avoid scams. Compare rates and fees before making a decision.

Prepaid Travel Cards: Another option to consider is using prepaid travel cards. These cards allow you to load money onto them in your home currency and use them like a debit card abroad. They often have lower or no foreign transaction fees, making them a convenient and cost-effective option.

Avoid Cell Phone Roaming Charges

When traveling to Ecuador, it's important to be mindful of cell phone roaming charges to prevent unexpected expenses and stay connected without breaking the bank. Here are some tips to avoid roaming charges:

Check with Your Service Provider: Contact your cell phone service provider before your trip to inquire about international roaming plans. They may offer temporary packages or options to minimize roaming charges. Be sure to clarify the terms, coverage, and costs associated with these plans.

Use Local SIM Cards: Consider purchasing a local SIM card upon arrival in Ecuador. This allows you to have a local phone number and access local rates for calls, texts, and data. Ensure your phone is unlocked and compatible with the local network.

Utilize Wi-Fi: Take advantage of Wi-Fi hotspots available in hotels, cafes, and public areas. Use messaging apps, VoIP services, and social media platforms to communicate with friends and family instead of making costly international calls or sending text messages.

Offline Maps and Apps: Download offline maps and travel apps before your trip. This allows you to navigate and access information without requiring a constant data connection. Pre-download any necessary maps, translation apps, or travel guides to avoid using data while on the go.

Enable Airplane Mode: To prevent unintentional data usage, activate Airplane Mode on your phone when you don't need to make or receive calls or use data services. This ensures your device won't connect to any roaming networks.

Consider an Ecuador SIM Card or Mifi Device

When traveling to Ecuador, one of the best ways to stay connected and avoid excessive roaming charges is by considering the use of an Ecuador SIM card or MiFi device. Here's why:

Cost Savings: Purchasing a local SIM card in Ecuador allows you to access local rates for calls, texts, and data. It can significantly reduce your expenses compared to using your home country's SIM card with international roaming. Local SIM cards often offer affordable data packages, making it convenient to stay connected without breaking the bank.

Convenience: With an Ecuador SIM card, you'll have a local phone number, which makes it easier for locals to contact you and for you to communicate within the country. You can make local calls, send texts, and use data services seamlessly.

Flexibility: By having a local SIM card, you have the freedom to choose from various mobile network providers and select the plan that best suits your needs. You can easily top up your credit or purchase data packages according to your usage.

MiFi Devices: Alternatively, you can consider renting or purchasing a MiFi device in Ecuador. A MiFi device acts as a portable Wi-Fi hotspot, allowing you to connect multiple devices simultaneously. This is especially useful if you're traveling with a group or if you require constant internet access for work or navigation purposes.

Download Offline Map

When traveling to Ecuador, it's highly recommended to download offline maps to ensure you have access to navigation even when you don't have an internet connection. Here's why downloading offline maps is beneficial:

Access Without Data or Wi-Fi: Offline maps allow you to navigate and explore Ecuador without relying on a constant data or Wi-Fi connection. This is particularly useful when you're in remote areas or when you want to conserve data usage.

Save Data and Roaming Charges: By using offline maps, you can avoid using your mobile data or incurring roaming charges for navigation purposes. This helps you stay within your data plan limits and prevents any unexpected charges.

Reliable Navigation: Offline maps provide reliable navigation even in areas with weak or no network coverage. You can rely on the downloaded maps for accurate directions, points of interest, and information about nearby attractions.

Plan Ahead and Explore Offline: By downloading offline maps, you can plan your itinerary in advance and explore without the need for an internet connection. You can mark important locations, find nearby restaurants or landmarks, and navigate confidently.

To download offline maps, you can use popular mapping applications such as Google Maps, MAPS.ME, or Here WeGo. These apps allow you to select specific regions or areas of Ecuador to download and access offline. Remember to download the maps when you have a stable internet connection before your trip.

Ecuadorian Useful Phrases and Local Customs

When visiting Ecuador, it's helpful to familiarize yourself with some useful phrases and local customs to enhance your cultural experience and communicate effectively with locals. Here are a few key phrases and customs to keep in mind:

Greetings: Start conversations with a warm greeting like "Buenos días" (good morning), "Buenas tardes" (good afternoon), or "Buenas noches" (good evening). Shake hands or give a light kiss on the cheek when meeting someone.

"Por favor" and "Gracias": These phrases, meaning "please" and "thank you," are universally appreciated and show politeness. Use them when making requests or expressing gratitude.

"¿Cómo estás?" and "¿Cómo te llamas?": These phrases, meaning "How are you?" and "What's your name?" can help initiate friendly conversations and show interest in getting to know people.

"Disculpe" and "Perdón": Use these phrases to apologize or politely ask for someone's attention.

"¡Salud!": When sharing a meal or having a drink, it's customary to say "Salud!" which means "Cheers!"

Respect for Indigenous Customs: In Indigenous communities, it's important to show respect for their traditions and customs. Ask for permission before taking photos, be mindful of cultural practices, and always follow any instructions given by community members.

Dress Code: When visiting churches or religious sites, it's respectful to dress modestly and cover your shoulders and knees. Additionally, some restaurants and establishments may have a dress code, so it's a good idea to dress appropriately.

CONCLUSION

Ecuador is a captivating destination that offers a rich blend of natural wonders, cultural heritage, and warm hospitality. From the breathtaking Andean Highlands to the lush Amazon Rainforest and the pristine Galápagos Islands, Ecuador's diverse landscapes never fail to leave visitors in awe. The country's vibrant history, indigenous traditions, and flavorful cuisine add to its allure, making it a truly unique and rewarding travel destination.

Whether you're an adventure seeker, nature lover, history buff, or culture enthusiast, Ecuador has something to offer for everyone. The stunning natural landscapes provide ample opportunities for outdoor activities such as hiking, biking, wildlife encounters, and birdwatching. Exploring indigenous communities and learning about their customs and rituals offers a chance to delve into the rich cultural heritage of the country.

Additionally, Ecuador's vibrant cities, such as Quito and Cuenca, are home to charming colonial architecture, bustling markets, and vibrant art scenes. Visitors can immerse themselves in the local culture, visit museums and art galleries, and indulge in traditional crafts and cuisine.

With its friendly locals, affordable options, and an abundance of attractions, Ecuador is a destination that can be enjoyed by travelers of all budgets and preferences. Whether you're seeking adventure, relaxation, or cultural immersion, Ecuador will leave a lasting impression and create memories that will stay with you long after your journey ends.

FAQ

Q: Is it safe to travel to Ecuador?
A: Ecuador is generally a safe country to visit, but it's always important to exercise caution and take common-sense precautions. Be aware of your surroundings, avoid displaying valuable items, and stay updated on the current safety situation in the areas you plan to visit.

Q: What is the currency in Ecuador?
A: The currency in Ecuador is the US dollar. It is recommended to carry smaller denominations and have some change on hand for convenience.

Q: Do I need a visa to visit Ecuador?

A: Visitors from many countries, including the United States, Canada, the United Kingdom, and most European Union countries, do not need a visa to enter Ecuador for tourism purposes. However, it's essential to check visa requirements based on your nationality before traveling.

Q: What is the best time to visit Ecuador?

A: Ecuador's weather varies depending on the region, so the best time to visit depends on your interests. The dry season, from June to September, is generally considered the best time for outdoor activities and exploring the Galápagos Islands. The Amazon Rainforest and coastal regions have a more tropical climate year-round.

Q: Can I drink tap water in Ecuador?

A: It is generally recommended to drink bottled water in Ecuador to avoid any potential stomach issues. Bottled water is readily available for purchase.

Q: What should I pack for my trip to Ecuador?

A: Packing essentials include comfortable walking shoes, lightweight clothing, a hat, sunscreen, insect repellent, a rain jacket, and a power adapter for electrical outlets.

Q: What languages are spoken in Ecuador?

A: The official language of Ecuador is Spanish. However, in indigenous communities, various native languages are spoken.

Leave a Review

Thank you for taking the time to explore the Ecuador Travel Guide. If you found this book helpful in planning your trip or if it provided valuable insights during your visit to Ecuador, I encourage you to leave a review on Amazon. Your review can greatly assist other travelers like yourself in discovering this informative resource.

By sharing your experience and thoughts, you can contribute to the travel community and help others make informed decisions about their own adventures in Ecuador. Whether it's highlighting the comprehensive information, the captivating storytelling, or the practical tips provided, your review can make a difference.

Additionally, if you're an avid traveler seeking more destination guides, I invite you to check out the "Roaming Nomad Series" books on Amazon by Melissa J Norman. This series offers a wide range of country-specific travel guides, each filled with unique insights, captivating stories, and practical advice to enhance your travel experiences.

Your support and feedback are invaluable, not only for this book but for future travelers who are looking for reliable and engaging resources. Leaving a review is a simple yet impactful way to give back to the travel community and help fellow explorers make the most of their journeys.

Thank you for considering leaving a review, and I hope you continue to explore the "Roaming Nomad Series" books for your future travel endeavors. Happy travels!

Additional Travel Resources

In addition to the valuable information provided in this travel guide, there are several other resources that can enhance your travel experience in Ecuador.

Travel Websites and Blogs: Explore popular travel websites and blogs dedicated to Ecuador. These platforms offer a wealth of firsthand travel experiences, tips, and recommendations from fellow travelers who have visited the country. They can provide insights on lesser-known attractions, off-the-beaten-path destinations, and personal anecdotes that can help you plan your itinerary.

Travel Forums and Online Communities: Join online travel forums and communities where you can ask questions, seek advice, and connect with other travelers who have been to Ecuador. These platforms allow you to interact with experienced travelers, gain insider tips, and gather up-to-date information about local customs, transportation, accommodations, and more.

Local Guidebooks: Consider investing in comprehensive guidebooks dedicated to Ecuador. These guidebooks provide detailed information on attractions, maps, historical context, cultural insights, and practical tips. They can be handy companions during your trip, allowing you to delve deeper into the country's rich heritage and discover hidden gems.

Travel Apps: Download travel apps that can assist you during your time in Ecuador. From language translation apps to navigation tools, currency converters, and virtual maps, these apps can make your travel experience more convenient and efficient.

Contact Information

For any additional questions or inquiries related to your travel to Ecuador, it's important to have access to relevant contact information. Here are some key contacts to keep in mind:

Embassy/Consulate: Find the contact details of your country's embassy or consulate in Ecuador. They can provide assistance in case of emergencies, provide travel advisories, and offer support in case of any issues during your trip.

Tourist Information Centers: Locate the nearest tourist information center in the city or region you are visiting. They can provide you with maps, brochures, and updated information about attractions, events, and local services.

Local Emergency Numbers: Save the local emergency numbers in Ecuador, including the police, ambulance, and fire department. In case of any emergencies, these numbers will be crucial for immediate assistance.

Accommodation Contact Details: Keep the contact information of your hotel or accommodation readily available. This includes their phone number, email address, and physical address. In case of any changes to your reservation or if you require assistance during your stay, you can easily reach out to them.

Transportation Providers: Note down the contact information for transportation providers such as airlines, bus companies, and car rental agencies. Having their contact details handy can help you with any travel-related inquiries or changes to your itinerary.

Maps and City Guides: Navigating Ecuador's Cities and Regions

Navigating the cities and regions of Ecuador is made easier with the help of maps and city guides. These invaluable resources provide essential information, detailed maps, and insightful tips to help you explore and navigate the country with confidence.

Maps: Whether you prefer physical maps or digital options, having a map of Ecuador is crucial for understanding the layout of cities, identifying landmarks, and planning your routes. Maps highlight major roads, attractions, neighborhoods, and important points of interest, allowing you to navigate efficiently and make the most of your time.

City Guides: City guides provide comprehensive information about specific cities in Ecuador. They offer insights into the local culture, history, attractions, dining, and entertainment options. With detailed descriptions and recommendations, these guides help you discover hidden gems, popular sights, and local favorites. They often include suggested itineraries, walking tours, and tips on public transportation, making it easier to explore independently.

Additionally, many city guides offer practical information such as transportation maps, restaurant guides, and accommodation recommendations. They provide a wealth of knowledge about the city's unique characteristics, allowing you to immerse yourself in the local atmosphere and make the most of your visit.

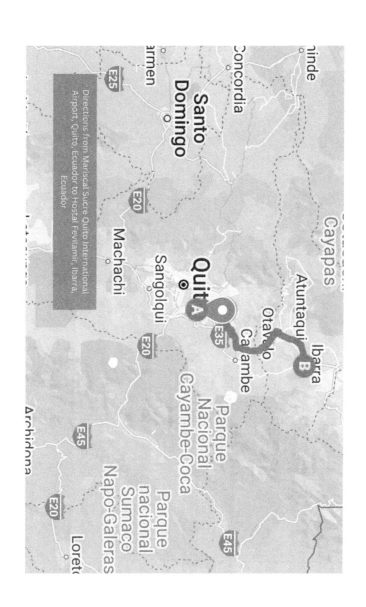

Directions from Mariscal Sucre Quito International Airport, Quito, Ecuador to Hostal Fevilamir, Ibarra, Ecuador

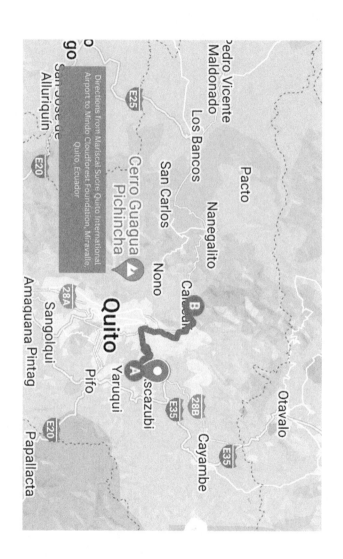

Directions from Mariscal Sucre Quito International Airport to Mindo Cloudforest Foundation, Miravalle, Quito, Ecuador

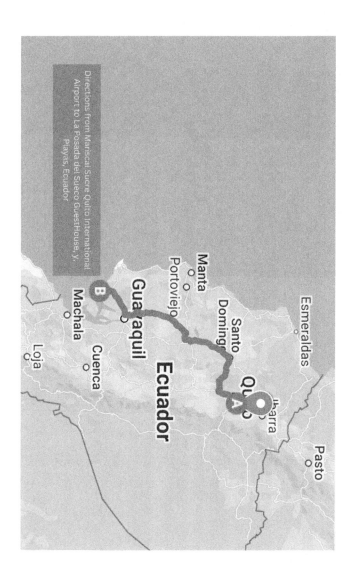

Directions from Mariscal Sucre Quito International Airport to La Posada del Sueco GuestHouse, y., Playas, Ecuador

125

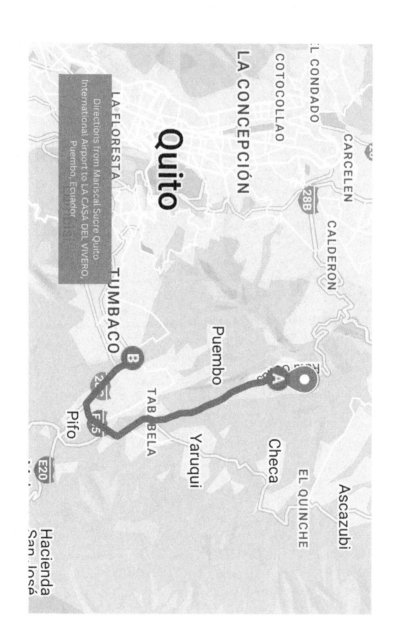

Directions from Mariscal Sucre Quito International Airport to LA CASA DEL VIVERO, Puembo, Ecuador.

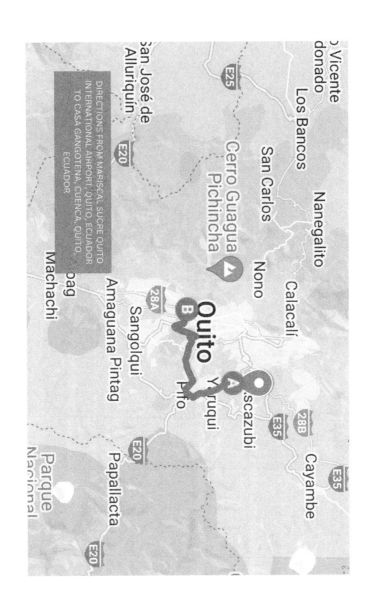

DIRECTIONS FROM MARISCAL SUCRE QUITO
INTERNATIONAL AIRPORT, QUITO, ECUADOR
TO CASA GANGOTENA, CUENCA, QUITO,
ECUADOR

127

Directions from Mariscal Sucre Quito International Airport, Quito, Ecuador to Hacienda Zuleta, Angochagua, Imbabura Province, Ecuador

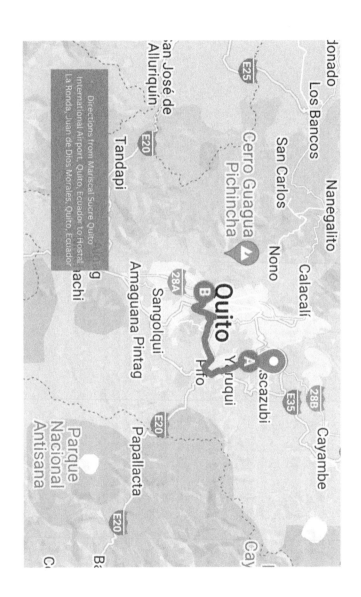

Directions from Mariscal Sucre Quito International Airport, Quito, Ecuador to Hostal La Ronda, Juan de Dios Morales, Quito, Ecuador
Los Bancos
San Carlos
Nanegalito
Cerro Guagua Pichincha
Nono
Calacalí
Quito
Sangolquí
Amaguana Pintag
Tandapi
Alluriquín
Pifo
Cayambe
Papallacta
Parque Nacional Antisana
E25
E20
28A
E35
28B
A
B

Printed in Great Britain
by Amazon

26370991R00076